ROAD TO REFLECTION

BYPASS ROAD TO NOWHERE

JAMES R. SANER II

Road to Reflection
Copyright © 2014 by James R. Saner II. All rights reserved.

No part of this publication may be reproduced, stored in a retrieval system or transmitted in any way by any means, electronic, mechanical, photocopy, recording or otherwise without the prior permission of the author except as provided by USA copyright law.

Published in the United States of America

ISBN: 9798306571089
1. Poetry / American / General
2. Philosophy / Mind & Body
14.03.22

I would like to thank The Creator for the Blessings in my life: My Wife, Children, Parents, Grandparents, and Relatives.

Family is truly the greatest Treasures of the Here and After.

I Am a Child

Child like words
Child like manners,
The hint to the answer
I am a child
I am a child!
Scared
Frightened by the futures arrival!
I am a child grown up now,
I am an adult,
I am scared of growing old.
I look back
Searching for my childhood,
Almost forgotten
But still in the process of!

Memories Reflected Upon

To the mountains rock of ages,
To the mother earth we praise you.
To the oceans from which we came
To the Heavens, the skies of space.
The time in which we began,
The time in which we end
A stream of conscious motion
The seasons, Summer, Falls, Winter, Springs
To life painting the landscapes a magnificent white.
The hour glass of time,
Deserts forming on the inside.
Keeping track of memories reflected upon.

James R. Saner II

My Queen

Give me your love,
And you give me heaven.
Share with me your life,
And I will listen.
Whisper in my ear your sweet nothings
And I will whisper in yours I love you .
If you fall in love with me I will be happy,
I will be your brightest star throughout all of Heaven.
We will grow together searching for some destination,
Something called love, understanding, and wisdom.
All we need is trust
Hope in each other.
We will have beautiful children who will grow up
Free and brilliant,
Connected to the creation and it's creator.
Listen to your heart,
Let your soul come out and touch me.
I love you forever!
My queen.

Road to Reflection

To The One I Love

These times are hard and dreary without you
I am lost and unhappy.
To the one I love,
The days are passing by don't forget me,
For I am waiting to be with you.
As time passes I am growing weak,
For the one I love is gone.
But the one I miss most is you.
For all the time we spent together,
For all the pain and sorrow you went through.
I was always with you.
But the worst was death,
The end to life as people see it.
The long dark path most people choose to take,
Hoping strongly, I wish you to look upon the light,
and find your place in time, where rest and peace are made easy.
With your help after death I too have gained the light
And I am looking forward in seeing you there, alive.
To the one I love.

James R. Saner II

1.7- 5.1 Million

Where is the rule that's so golden,
Did you forget who wrote it,
Maybe gave it to one of the other poets
Or lost it?
Someone knows
Lisa and Howard
Don't forget Elizabeth
Playing money games with the gifted.
Take a trip to the good old Capital,
See good old talk show host Montel,
This is funny
This is amazing
How things can change
Feeling a little crazy,
Receiving the same thing
Having the same chance to win as 1.7 million.

A Type

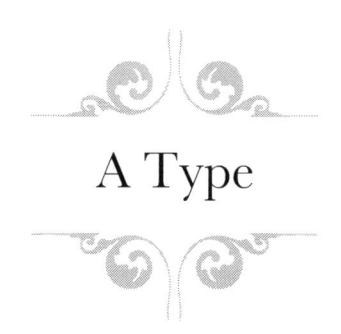

What type are you?
Yep, some kind of type-
A type like any other,
Just one of them things
Yep, kind of type things you see
On the movie screen/computer-
Radio signal shared by all
The viewers.
What you see?
Was it some kind of type thing.
Journal on somebody's page
Web of communication,
Bring me the link
And connect me to the transmitter...
A Type,
Blood is thicker, red wine.

James R. Saner II

Addict

So much for the last time,
I keep on doing it.
The next time is the last time,
Until the next after that one
Doing it and not willing to give it up,
But wanting to be at that point.
Not just in this case but many others
Continued race for the best,
Feeling like this is it,
But it's not,
Addict can't give it up,
Hopeless lost cause of life,
Kicked to the side
Left to die, without knowing why
They do it.

Again

Again
And again
And again it goes,
Again
And again
And again it goes,
Again
And again
And again it grows
Again
And again
And again it knows
What this time is all about Who
knows?

James R. Saner II

Age to Come

Ways away from time
Already passed by the longing
For love, with its affections
Landing somewhere close to home
The heart opens wide
Smiling
Warmth of the body
Trust in mind
True love of mine
Shine as the morning comes.
As we begin and so it ends
Faster than when it started,
The wheel keeps turning,
With the symbol of progress
Moving closer to the Age to come-
Future is seen only in dream,
For that is what makes us.

Road to Reflection

All The Same Thing

Problem to be solved,
Question is to find the formula,
And have the answer
Without knowing the pieces to the problem
Letter of physical mass structure
Outside the human body in the spirit
Of one individual-
Possible to be shared with others
Only by intent
Or will
Spirit kind of energy
Worlds of great links
Connecting vast amounts of beings
All the same thing.
Now how is that possible?

James R. Saner II

Already Proven

When we have a chance
we take it,
Or do we?
Well maybe we should
Someday
Some way it will happen
And if it doesn't,
So be it,
No time to waste
To short is life
Not to live,
The game is the same
Only one solution-
It doesn't stop until you're dead,
Already proven!

Basic Smoke

Basic art of living as we must, maintain
Our standard, Basic depths to the human soul
Reject the outcome for it is hollow.
Cry no more, Sky above is fading...
Into the spaces images we run unbalanced
Singing praises for the son..
Vision lost by lack of light giving in
To the darkness of night,
Cast me into the deep cool tunnel
Wait for me so that I am not alone
Over the horizon here it comes.
Lost art of basic principle
To touch it with my tongue
And to feel it through my body
Having it all for myself,
It is something to love the warmth
When it comes up I can see the image
Of light, feel it battle the chill of
My body. Then the wait for night begins
All over... Basic smoke.

James R. Saner II

Beautiful One

Stand proud
Beautiful one,
See the clouds
Blocking the sun,
Walk on water child
Don't be afraid to go any higher..
Love tall
Beautiful one,
Love them all
Beautiful one.
The Dreams they are alive
Living next door to the theatre.

Blind Man

The blind man
Sees spiritually
Everything
Travels like me,
His name is James like me,
Gave me my spiritual name:
Sky wolf.
A gift to heal like me.
Shaman,
The great spiritual medicine man.
Holy is
Holy was
Holy will be,
Spirit manifestation.

James R. Saner II

Body of The Mind

Enter
Says the sign,
One way through the mind
Take your time
Many different thoughts
The Universal Library,
Stay on the path
Follow the arrows
Or lose yourself in an endless maze,
The Body Of The Mind
Keep your faith
Allow yourself to find the exit
Escape, you're safe
until you realize you're in another mind
All time ongoing never are you through
At all times entering and exiting-

Road to Reflection

Breaking Dawn

Silently the night is
Then the breaking of the dawn,
The world humming like a machine
Spirits in bodies rising in form to
Come together as the masses,
This intelligence knowing there is
Higher yet still to come
Downward
Upward, waves of perception
Something's always better
This it understands not,
But has to accept it
The sky above begins to fill with light blue colors,
Breaking Dawn winds, bring up the sun...

James R. Saner II

Burning Peace

What would you call this
If nobody told you what this was
To be sure enough about your communication
Heart beating drum sounds like amazing,
Pattern in the mind in bed a sleep
Lost in it all the ghost keeps on
Breathing, pretending to still be alive
Living as if this still has meaning
Can't be real if it isn't I say
Leave the people alone and watch it burn
Damn walls of flames colors swirl in vision
Crystal ship Leaving port-

Child

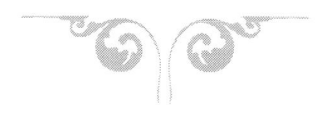

Growing we grow inside ourselves,
Another part of the almighty being
Spirit dancing in the soul, rejoice
For the lost sheep.
Sleep my child in rest and peace
The days slip into another dream,
May laughter fill your heart
And may joy lead your life,
For your father is but a guide.
I am but a simple little part,
Of who you truly are,
By faith you will know thy self.
You asked me to give you life,
I did as you wished now grow
My child into the spirit of love.

James R. Saner II

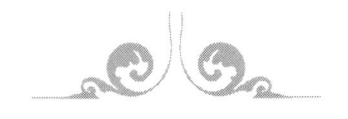

Down The Hole

Deep down the hole we go
black thickens to lose control
Covering over the pupils
Invading light particles
Splitting the senses
Breath gone no more to draw
The passage into who we are,
Deep down the hole we go
No more power no more home,
Entering into the world
Spirit flaming wanting to over take its
Vessel, leaving the others
In darkness.
The birth happens here we are
Free to do with life what we want
After that coming back to the black hole,
Deep down the hole we go, this time
Dirt is put on top of us
Closing the passage time stands still
Yet the movement is constant.

Road to Reflection

Eternal Bliss

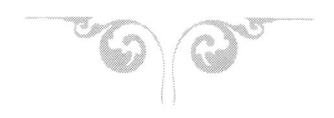

Welcome mat sits to the side of the door
Feet walking in stride
Wiped on as the visitors` voice says hello
I have come to your house to share
The good news, that in fact he is here.
The creator is coming to save the people
From themselves showing them the truth
Bringing the new way of living to
This very home,
Inside this heart lives the light
The love of peace and joy
The American Prayer
Black as the American Night
Shadows of time and lives once lived
The being is constant
Eternal Bliss!

James R. Saner II

Fallen Angel

Falling angels out of the realm,
Falling into lonely calm.
The morning star gone from the creator
Out of reach from open arms,
Lost forgotten child.
Blamed for all that is wrong.
My fault my fault
Burn in hell for all
Falling from grace and love
Farther yet still
more to come
Fall Lucifer fall
No hope at all
Just you alone to take the fall
Create God for us all,
Maybe Heaven maybe Hell
Which do you own?
None! You're just a fallen Star…

Free Is Nothing Any More

Crazy in life
Lost cause
Worth more than all, not for pride
Money, sex-
Honored is the love,
Bright shining future
Protected by the present,
Our being in Now
Free is nothing any more.
Prices go up, people still pay,
Giving it their all until
It's not enough.
Yet they keep paying.
Faith does this to the soul.

James R. Saner II

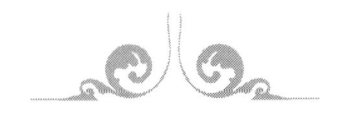

Freedom of Expression—ESCAPE!

The talent of ours—
He who takes the bread out of a young child's hands go & be filled,
you taught that child a lesson, how not to be when they grow old,
then they either boy or girl will teach the young a lesson of sharing, caring, giving—Forever more.
Then so on and so on, the generations go on!
The voice—The piano—The music of the soul.
The words—The rhythms—The beat—The message as they speak.
What is that spectacular noise.
How do they do it? Wow!
It's magic—A miracle—It's creative.
Inspired by something or just a relief—A mistake.
No way something great—Evolution or growth of the age,
Freedom
Of
Expression—ESCAPE!

Road to Reflection

Gentle Flesh

When it seems to slip away, that is
When you get the better view.
Cast into the shadow was the light,
Being small is better than small.
Different views of sort
Get inside have a look at the inners
Doctor mad at science
Savior
Gentle flesh
Bless you too
Give me what I want in paradise,
That is what it is
The Truth,
Good-Bye.

James R. Saner II

Ghost child

Crashed, left to die no reason why
Working fine earlier.
Later after the fire was controlled
Is when I first heard it, the sound in
A dream is something crazy
Buzzing in the inner ear
Ghost child led the people in a trance
To dance ancient wisdom
Healing no more mystery to me
The people I see are losing it.
Faith floating away like it was,
Unreal to some maybe to others
Not so real anymore.
Going home with the memories of
Yesterday which reflected the image
Of two days from now. Will I ever
See the day Freedom comes my way?
Probably already missed it…

Road to Reflection

Going Gone

Into the woods we go,
Cutting into the wildlife
Rewriting history, rough draft
To final
Revision lost in a daze a maze
Gone is whatever was before
Now is no more
Locked are the churches doors,
God's house open only on Sundays
Poor people sweat blood giving it
Their all,
While the rich people prophet off it,
No real middle class
Only divisions of some petty order,
Humans we think we know so much
What happens, is what we know goes—
Going gone.

James R. Saner II

Grand Review

Do you accept my challenge,
Can you live with the outcome
Do you have a choice
Or is it fate that speaks for you.
No more sacrifice in my name,
Death leaves my press alone
To give grand reviews.
The media money pool,
Small price for such news,
Not at this moment
Taken off the air
Making sure communication waves,
Are pure,
Political science
Down to the Q.

Heaven of Your Being

How long will I have to wait?
Bleeding heart.
All the love that is
I would give to be loved.
Burning attraction
Soul friend.
Who floods my thoughts.
I asked the question-
It takes a great deal to get my attention,
Yet I am enchanted by your total beauty.
Your eyes smile,
Your lips swell with passion-
Innocent touch
Sexuality
The Heaven of your Being.

James R. Saner II

Historic Human Suicide!

To the last great thing—
To know no consciousness
Swimming in a pool without water
To have no belief
Lost in the darkness of an underground cave
To go on living without love
Diving out of an airplane without a parachute
To give up hope
Driving 100mph towards a brick wall without your seatbelt on
To not strive for the future
Baring the past as if it never happened at all
A slow Death—They say
Is a longer life
Tactics used to destroy oneself
Historic Human Suicide!

Inner Most Depths

Water comes in great lengths
To overcome the banks,
Fluid moving in on trust
Better get back over to the far side
Look how still the ice is
Chilled to the inner most depths
This liquid was solid
Melted yes vapor gas sunny side
Up there over the hill down the
Trail we go then, rest is best
When tired.
Like the great Warning signs read
When you learn how to, listen not with
The ears but the mind's eye, take
A look at what's coming for you—-

James R. Saner II

Invisible

To all I see!!!!!!!!!
Invisible.
You can see me.
But I am invisible
Impossible to see me I am camouflaged by the trees,
The breeze,
Which ever setting you see
I Am In
But you can't see me like I said,
I am invisible,
I have special powers
Gifted.
I can see you
You are visible, but that doesn't mean you can see me!
I am like a Guardians Angel watching you and
Protecting you from Unknown problems
Like a God!

Island of Our Minds

Grown to know what it is,
The kind of knowing you get out of nowhere
But somewhere unknown
The Island of our minds the vast timeless
Inner, quick to remember, something long
Ago, stranger days I'm aware are coming
More and more often than before
Wait just a second something like a thousand
Years
Do you remember?–Unknown.

James R. Saner II

It is Yours

Take it if it means that much to you,
Be gentle with it after it is yours,
Don't wait around for someone to give it
To you,
Take charge and go
Through our actions and through our lives
We have many goals don't wait for them
To be given to you,
They are meant to be yours.
The ability to achieve comes from hard work
Focus on what is important,
Stand firm in your belief and knock on
Heaven's door
It is yours.

It Matters Not

It matters not what is said,
Only matters what is done,
Taking the chance at face value
Believing in the system
Trusting that all will work
That everything will be well
Coming together to take on the problem,
Not letting the truth be hidden
Making sure it is revealed,
Justice is a mocking thing
Can be purchased with power and money
Big scam of the day
The people are brain washed into thinking
They are free, learning someone else's
History and being introduced to the mass Machine.

James R. Saner II

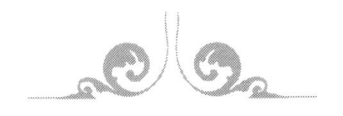

Just About Anything-

How true is this society as it stands,
Is the main theme money.
Just about anything-
What will be will be
Maybe this is true,
Going around in the name as if we are one,
Only postage stamped mail
Sent back to you, Poets society
Yes sir,
I feel close to you
Best be kept at a safe distance.
Like a drug is writing
Addiction to meaning
Blank lines represent the beginning.

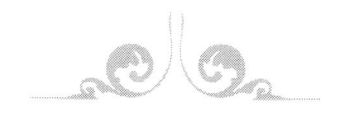

Landing Head First

Say did you
What
Such words
Scrambled worlds Over easy
Extra crispy
Cow cooked mooooooooo
Pig jumped over Jupiter's
Fourth moon,
Landing head first
Into mud
Frog laughed
Funny hah
Female Dear fawn
Chess master
King took pawn
Queen knocked kings
Socks off
Feet got cold during the night
Lasted to long soon to be forgotten,
Lost cause.

James R. Saner II

Let It Flow

Life winds blow, Human beings let it flow,
Space Distance Education,
The simple focus Breath.
The heart beat.
Touch energy
Touch being.
Live for it.
Live for that
Live for this.
Split person,
The base for freedom...

Life Underwriter

National look into the clouds,
Rain died down long ago,
Snow the white stuff all around,
Beautiful.
Let me live to see the day,
Then let the night take me.
Cast into the darkness with all my
Sin, let me sing to the Alpha
Do I not deserve to die for all the
Wrong I've done and for the hurt
I cast on others?
Just like the complete journal of
Man,
The life underwriter
Has gone on to the great council
Saying forgive him
He is just some petty fool.

James R. Saner II

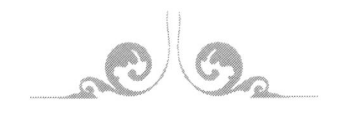

Limits Are Petty

Damn the rule
Its limits are petty
Social gatherings
Bring with them head aches
Past life dreams
Visions of walking
The sick waiting
For their medicine
All that is
Which is ancient
with out imitation
surely beyond the limits
They will to receive healing
Or to heal.

Little Secret

Missing words on the page,
Blank minded people.
Lost in a thought of not thinking
Something about something else,
Oh well, oh hell, not this story
I should say, all knowing what
A funny thing a game of lots played
For money,
Check the charge
Cards please, three of them
All different names,
Then we see who is who,
Just another bird man
Going someplace to tell
A secret to the god of past
And all. Eyes of the creatures
Spill much to the viewers
Not as if we already didn't know that
We were being watched by the god,
Little secret.. Shhhhhhhhhhhhhhh

James R. Saner II

Lust Isn't Love

Place of belonging
Taking care of hot desires,
Flaunting lust as if it were love
Amounting to depths of depression.
Nothing's left to be received
Greed builds up overwhelming
The breed of man, species
Looking out of the technical world
And into something that scares them
Natural.

No power lines

The Land of my childhood,
The Land of Shawnee, Hills and rivers
Native American Center Of The Universe
My blood with its flesh are of this land
Power dwells deep within the caves
Once there was no power lines with lights
Over roads, just the glow of the moon
In completion
New it is the darkness of night
No city lights, gone
Taken by the officials
Turned off,
To what it is we really are
Part of the darkness.

James R. Saner II

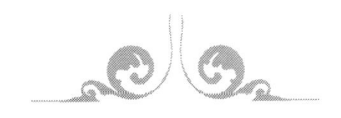

No Purchase Necessary!

Trapped in time,
All my thoughts rhyme,
How am I supposed to know?
Who I am,
Where I came from.
Who,
Who,
The owl!
The bird!
The oak tree.
Me
Everything!
All I see
The feelings.
Space
Free
No Purchase Necessary!

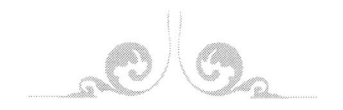

Not of the Flesh & Blood

My soul called out to my body
Letting me know that it's here
Whispers
Echoes
Ghosts
Spirits
Not of The Flesh & Blood
Presence
Comfortable
But scared you might be talking with someone
Privacy invaded on
Space explored
Who knows who you are?
My body cries out Freedom!

James R. Saner II

Observation From Above

Looking down from the skies above,
Viewing the ant hill of us,
Seeing a view point
Not always seen,
I am small in the real thing.
Little human ants keeping busy
Trying to have responsibility.
Up here life is relaxing,
Not imposing on me.
See the deal is this,
You think god is up here watching,
Judging what he sees
The queen ant of something,
Invisibility.

On This Page

On this page,
You have in front of you I leave
A book
Marking the faith to this life,
Shared long enough
To know what freedom is,
Time just goes by like clock work, In
Some other direction,
Caught off guard by aging,
Into the many places we go,
And for the ones we don't- pictures,
As part of the winds I feel
Its breath breathing instant fresh
Life here.
My fate is before the altar, Holy
Sainthood, Universal law.

James R. Saner II

Open space

Lost out in the open space of time
The child plays and prays his rhyme
Wishing for the end to begin
Opened doors into the future
Tomorrow seems so distant
Past sometime back over his shoulder
Cares not of either moment,
Being is something of constant structure
Movement out of the realm will cause
Non-existence.
Lost out in the open space of time
The child plays and prays his rhyme
Wishing for the beginning to end...

Road to Reflection

Power of Value

Power that walks behind you,
Power that is you
Growing into the self
Power of the source
Power being what it is
as natural
Healing being what it is
Power in the choice of our magic.
Words are power
So is voice
To sing the last great verse
The sounds of poetry
Betrayed by publication
Anything and everything
Power of Value limited by fools.

James R. Saner II

Remember

Why am I so afraid of leaving
Letting go,
Just disappearing?
Too scared to accept who I am and what I'm capable of.
Frightened when you realize the universe is really yours.
It's scary
When it's real.
God's gift (Words) mine and yours.
Come with me!
Share with me your story
I am listening.
Can you believe it, I created God,
In the same way he created me. Partners,
Friends, Freedom in the forest and the leaf caught in the wind.
Free to explore it,
The beginning, The end!
I love life and cherish its secrets.
They are my own and I am theirs.
Why did I choose to forget?
The only answer I came up with is to- Remember.

Road to Reflection

Responsibility

The star collapsed, sending
star dust on its way, Mass floating in space,
Heading our way.
Human D-day!
If impact occurs, who knows where you're going,
Probably be thrown
out of your body,
Soul sent skyrocketing—
Across the universe.
A lonely eternity!
Eternity is yours, How you view it
is very important, It is never ending,
Neither are you, So find emotion
and us feeling to pull through.
You've read the same book Over and Over,
Trying to see past the words.
Addicted to solving
Someone else's mystery,
It's time to create your own
—Responsibility!

James R. Saner II

Right or Wrong

The Unknown Author,
Mystery in myself
Caught by others in time living as life
Continues it's movement
Masses join to form larger mass,
Catholics seem to be my saviors
Breathing breath of goodness
Back into my soul spirit,
Which has been fighting its way
Out of hell
Or something damn close to it,
The course of action
Is simply to be as I am
True without a second thought,
Giving what is needed to be given
No more questioning right or wrong

Rose

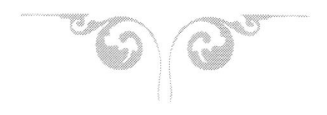

A rose is what lovers exchange when dating.
A flower that means something called love.
Love that is indescribable.
A feeling in one person's life trying to exchange with another.
But when the rose dies, we weep,
For it was an exchange of one person's feelings and emotions.
But the love of the rose will never die in one person's heart.
That's something that lasts forever,
Even after you die.
The rose is the only survivor.

James R. Saner II

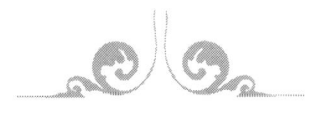

Rosehill Park

Lucky Day- The sign says Road Close,
No bridge
Yet seen is the other side of the road.
Divided Banks,
The creak floods with rage.
No Parking,
Park bench empty
Playground deserted,
Yellow slide,
Swings still swinging,
Ghostly winds.
Night settles in pushing the day farther west
Trees on the perimeter
Houses in the center
A thousand colors manifest
Peripheral vision.
Sighted
The clouds look heavy-
I can see their edges.

Shared Trade

With in the darkness
Beautiful light,
Always has it been in troubles
Ancient graph of elders
Stars on maps leading to the heavens door
Entrance is knowledge with a price fee of
all your sins
No cents allowed
Sin is a little over done
Claimed as the price on your head
Worth as much as what exactly?
Often wondered but only given
So much attention
Yet what is called life continues
Going like a code or connection
Of one simple thing,
Power of the business,
Shared trade of people

James R. Saner II

Sleep

Sleep in my love the world all over,
Sleep my drug of choice to give to all,
Special high how's it going
Fine
So true is life without the host
Cleaning the dishes for the party,
My members to be with me for so long.
Let us say farewell,
Good-bye to this world
So I might enter another
Sleep with in my love all is well
Sleep is deep the depth to shallow.
Sleep so true in rest and work to
Escape the labors of life we close
Our eyes and go.

So We Did

The people
Then we stand up
To the great unknown,
Moving on in time
Space growing and breathing
Around us,
Believing in the system
That captured us
Walking away from the devil,
Let the light shine
For all to see
Love and peace are free,
Healing spirit with in thee
My home is a part of me,
My temple walks with me,
We must find the holy city
The choice to see, grant we
As a people forgiveness-

James R. Saner II

Spirits Passion

Life has
but no end
Live as you must.
To testify
And not give into opinion
Faith flows much deeper.
The voice of man
Is the spirits passion
Love in always.
How you see
Is things change
A whiteness to all life!
To know something really
Exploring every reality of that
Which is your life!

Stay Alive

Stay alive when you die and see what's out
There
Death in its self a player
Fire dances from the sword
The realm of ancient answers
Name for your creator
Command
Cut into stone by thy flaming finger
Shot down to the soul
Taken back from utter darkness,
Coming straight into glowing light
It was
How you say blissful..

James R. Saner II

Stolen Dream

Shadows end
Leaving with the body,
wings of angels glowing
Gone again,
Stolen Dream
Destiny writing its message on the walls
Yourself mistaken for an image
Body strong lacking wisdom
Imprisoned with thyself
True this stolen dream seems real enough
But I ask you,
Is It?

Stop & Listen

For a minute without seconds,
Stop and listen for a spell.
Check the subject
Matter of fact
More than once is enough
Stop and listen
Patients is a must for hospitals
minding in view of shattered windows
How do people with nothing at all
Get weapons in their hands,
They are dropped off in vans
Left on the side street
Of the project
Possible to find the project owner
Same goes for all kinds of control,
There is a fog over us.

James R. Saner II

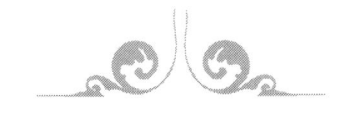

The Deeds Crusade

Pet the snake
Feed the lion
Train the beast
going wild
Out on the edge of town
The youth sing
Raising their voices to the skies
The winds blow harder
The sound grows louder
The invasion begins
The day becomes historical
Raise the dead to lament
While the living stop their breathing
To join the deeds crusade.

The Music

The Music Fills your soul Like the ancient river.
Danger is not
A loud entrance
In this most sacred place.
The Circle is around us
Protecting us,
And what you see is Unheard of!
The voice
You hear remains unseen.
Who is it? I don't know
The face of mystery.
The one who fights eternal death,
The savior of souls laid to rest.
Come
Follow me- the music is calling me
To walk the narrow road.
Not long till this journey has passed, and
There you will find your Path-
Today is really Tomorrow!

James R. Saner II

The Past Creeps Toward The Future

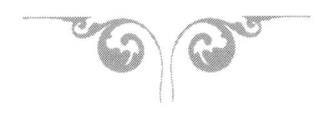

Lightning gas,
Bleeding energy!
Flash, Flash,
In a moment or two
Cost
The price!
Beg your pardon,
No sales this month.
Slow in the fast.
The Past creeps toward The Future.
Momentum Speed
Driving and Smiling.
Death to itself,
The present-
Now!
Now it is ready.
Time to sleep,
Time to rise,
Out of your dreams do come.

Road to Reflection

The Silent Story

Being still in silence
Letting the learned memory rest
Being still in silence
No life
No death
Breath deep the winds
Humming as it passes
Know this as it truly is
Being still in silence
Reality shifts like waves of radio AM/FM
They hear the song
Visions of the natives dance
Nations unite in circled courtship
Creating up rise in this
The silent story.

James R. Saner II

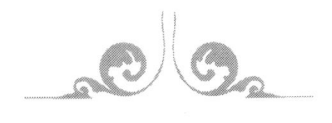

The Source

Then I am the master,
The sun shines on me—sunny.
Reflection doesn't show the smoke entering your lungs.
Perfect picture I'm glad I was in it.
It is my reflection, The skies are my ocean.
As the master I am the servant, The Host.
My reason why I'm here!
So nice to be alone and feel yourself.
The sun is bleeding through the clouds—our motion picture lens.
Too Hot
Touches us from a distance.
The Source,
The Light,
The Magic!

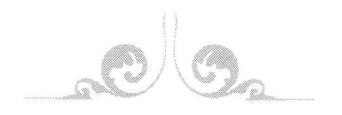

The Truth Is

The truth is, I'm just here.
No reason worth mentioning,
Unsure of how much to you.
Purpose,
Created by what,
Seen by what.
What is all these things.
Much
Life!
Much
Love!
Tapping into that,
Realizing that,
What is that.
Silence...
Reality is worth this,
As big as this reality was,
Is
Could be.
The truth is, I'm just here.

James R. Saner II

The Universe Shall Answer

In time the truth shall come about
Bringing with it understanding and wisdom,
Imagination shining bright and brilliant
For the children of ages past and present
Looking to the future for salvation,
The universe shall answer
Coming to the aid of this worlds victims,
Punishing the users of the peoples,
Forgiveness only goes for the ones who
Understand their wrong doings
Calling on the god or gods of ancient times this place
This time
Shall no longer be in existence.

The Wonder Of

Eyes looking direct
Focused on your vehicle, body
Dark as night itself these people wonder
What I am doing
Who do I think I am? Nobody
Questions in mind mistaken for thought,
Isn't it amazing the wonder of
Many different worlds in this the one,
How long ago was history
Not that far off to be forgotten
Civil rights
The wars to get here where we are.
This is not ours by right or law,
Taken by the government for property plots.

James R. Saner II

Then I Will

Man
Don't you know that I am spiritual.
Spirit in the Flesh.
How long do you think I will be here?
Doe's it matter?
Afraid are you of nothing.
I can't help that I care
About Wisdom and Knowledge.
The work it takes us all to get.
Life I'm afraid is more than nothing.
More in every view or judgment of it.
Please
If I could I would!
Then I Will.

Road to Reflection

This, That & the Other

This person I am being is me
Everything that I am
seeing is showing
Truth is moving like never before
Glowing dreaming as a child
As we go now
To the adult
The me that is the child
Running into what we call life
Really what it is-is the death
Life comes after
That is what we call this,
that and the other.

James R. Saner II

Touch the Spirit

Living in a made up world-
Lessons,
Work,
Preoccupation-
No time to learn,
Less time for patients.
Nothings happening
It wasn't expected,
Just came as coincidence
Gradually happened.
Look what we became!
Isn't it amazing
Our story is History,
Not just as a group but- Individually
We are images words on paper
That are spoken, Imagination, real & fiction.
Touch the spirit,
Become a part of it
That's the gateway
Open feelings
True form of meditation.
Peace
Your karma is happy.

Road to Reflection

Train 109!

Last call—
Train 109 leaving.
All aboard!
Soul Train just left the station,
You missed it.
Damn it!
Late again as usual!
O well,
I'll catch the next one.
When is it? Not till tomorrow.
What time? Evening Noon!
Not till midnight,
What am I supposed to do?
Catch it!
Same thing I told you last time,
You have to come sooner.
Or what I'll miss it?
Good conclusion!!!!

James R. Saner II

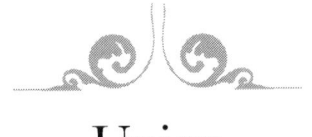

Union

Justice of the peace,
The symbol of well being,
Magical passage
Open window into which they climb
Over the edge of Freedom
Growth of a new dawn
A new Age
The Devil finished in the game
Thrown through the abyss.
The haven
Safe place called Heaven
Mortals let us in
We saw the union–
Father is Son, Son is Father,
Son IS father had a son
Who was everything.

Walk With You

Like me or not,
I have a way about myself,
Charm
Kindness for all who know me,
Listen for the wind to speak
Listen for the timeless me
Enter as one of these
Child and you shall have your peace.
Forgive as you wish to be,
Let I say have Forgiveness
Let my spirit walk with you
Accept my healing
It is Free,
You within me...

James R. Saner II

We Shall

Like so many others,
They struggle with themselves,
Lost inside not knowing much of anything
More than they could handle
Taking with them the spell
Cast over the shoulder of sleeping
Animals
For so long now the spirit has
Been missing,
given to the child as offering...
To the living and to the dead
Our heads hang down
In the remembrance of ourselves,
Something's going down
Shall we live to see it..
We shall...

What

Our world of poetry linked by energy,
glowing as if it were a dream
Learning how right you are
Poetry laughing in the face
of our humanity
To this very day
I still pray
I just don't tell anyone
Deep within the source my journey goes
Learning how to be saved by what
Silence is lost in noise but takes refuge
in still being there
Funny how many times it happens
And we just don't know
Seekers been there already and
They know what's What! -always...

James R. Saner II

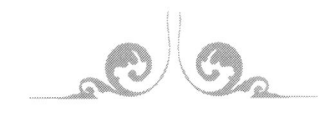

Where Is My Love?

In the hours unaware of, where does my love go?
Does it go to each and every one of you?
Filling you with the warmth and peacefulness that it does me.
Where is my love when life feels to heavy to bare;
Is it with you helping through the struggles of worldly life?
Is it just love?
Wherever you are, my love, I hope you feel me and miss me as I miss you, in this sorrow I can say that I know love.
For I will wait a thousand years if need be,
but please me, my love, wherever you are,
for I am lonesome and tired of being alone.
Where is my love when I am working, when I am sleeping, when I am gone?
Hopefully my love is true with me and will always search for me
until she can see me smile.
I am in love with you, my love, until the last breath leaves my lungs.
Then, if I can, I will continue to love you, my love.
Forever are my vows strong.

Road to Reflection

Wilderness

Grant me this time to do my thing and be my own somebody.
Free my life will be when you come to take me away
I will play on your note like a kid or goat
Escaping from the dark shadows of night
Entering the body of tomorrow,
Blessing my people as the holy man dances to bring healing
On like it were a breeze or something.
My breath leaving and coming all in a single motion
Like the ocean we are never still,
Till then we come inside ourselves locked away
In this vessel looking to be saved by a savior
But never by myself, animal part of our lives distinct nature
Captured and rebuilt like we believe in the master of our slavery,
Me in time will be let out to be seen by someone else,
Who is looking to be a spirit more than a man by reasonable nature.

James R. Saner II

Take the message that the messengers are still seeking to be heard
By the voices who just will not stop.
Gone is the end of my time last before the first
Brought on by the second coming of our evolution.
Seen clear for miles—Wilderness! More here than not.
Governed controlled environment.

Road to Reflection

Yes Is Good

Great is great,
Life is death or something close to it.
Imagine
Burned into my thinking like immortal sin.
Fear of
Yes is good
Something,
Is given
Only to be received...
SO Is this Word-
Go Means stop to some...
Lost somewhere in my thinking...

James R. Saner II

Untitled

Loss in every step,
Walking in the middle
Backwards I find myself looking inward
Reflection of an image spoken for,
Loss in the moment,
Hunted like a animal who's blood leaves
A trail for the predator, Coming!!!
Loss in this place,
Face I think I'm facing, not really me
But me in some twisted form, image of
Course,
Loss in time to get up again and again,
Never enough of, always up and down the sun
Goes,
Loss in aging process,
Just catch your breath man & be still
No way have to keep on with that
Growth till you choke and death has you,
Lost is this life I was born into
I forgot what it means to be...

Road to Reflection

Untitled

Of life and death
I must confess
I know not well
Found in darkness was my light source
Lost
Finding its way back home then
Tripped up in the matters of time
Energy got stuck in
Revolve the doors continue to spin,
entering is the way to exiting.
Freedom
of the mind
SOUL
Body
Escaping into unknown regions
The Great I AM....

James R. Saner II

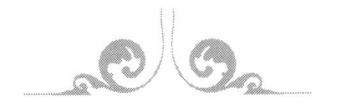

And There Are Many Doors

And there are many doors to open
Many minds to see
A lesson of travel
Plains to the seas
Circle upon circle
Mass to energy
The one true source, the only
ONE alone
Drifting Becoming
Another and another
One among many, Many in the One
And there are many doors
Many minds to wander
Only one Home
And now I have come & now I go
And then I open another Door
Jumped through the Windows,
Took a look at your soul
Light of being Your light of ME,
The only Host I know...

Road to Reflection

A Little Mouse

I have visited the small world &
found it to be really a large world,
all my favorite characters are there,
somebody had an idea
and voom look at all this stuff
celebrations the best here on earth,
Rides and parks
picture perfect world,
A journey really of our youth
a dive into the imagination
quest to go beyond today
and into the worlds of tomorrow
maybe on a little train or bus
maybe on a fairy boat
or up there in the clouds flying
in a plane without words I have become,
not so vocal am I any more
but wow my hats are off,
who would have thought a little mouse
could be worth so much.

James R. Saner II

A New Song

And a new song is born
as a gentle wind is blown
to and from
not so long
not too short
a story of a life
from crawling to walking
breathing to not
light in the dark
and a new song is song
to heal the sick & cure disease
perfection for the people
perfection in me
form
only one
and a child shall lead them
dancing & singing
and a new message has come...

Road to Reflection

A Structure (Part I.)

I walk through time the constant
Waking in mind
Caged inside the body
Energy or light
attracted to my opposite
Wanting to attune
Days and nights mix into one rotation
Depending on which side of the world your on
How fast it is going tic after tic
Constantly the seconds calculate and build
up in minutes to hours to days to weeks
To months to years to long
Who could have started this insane measure
Rotation after rotation
Beginning and ending in the same field of
light
Darkness
Shift in season new age
Old ONE.

James R. Saner II

A Structure (Part II.)

Forever in my trained mind
Thinking when I should not,
Quiet in the noise
The sound of a hummm
Drum
Heart beating until it doesn't
Learning the ways of the world
Learning the ways of the spirit
Power of the sums
Divided in my being
Drifting in the reason
Can't quite grasp the whole
Spell of things
Never ending spiral
Just changes after awhile
Taught to believe
When the action is against the Belief
it overcomes.

A Structure (Part III.)

When the humans started did we know what time was
Could we grasp the past
Present and Future of its constant body
A Structure
With different phases
Did we once believe that flight happened
In collective thought
To hard
Not hard enough
Truth misplaced in the face
The mirror image
Left becomes right
And the Blood Mary fright
Was I smarter as a child
Than I am as an adult
Did I lose something
Just gone for awhile...

James R. Saner II

A Wish Then to Condition the Soul (part I.)

So much for reason and the time we have,
In the blink of an eye children grown old
and the old soon to die,
So much for giving
I have nothing to give,
Life struggles hard and traps you in a cage
Puts you in a nice little box
And feeds you crumbs,
Enslaved to the grave & burdened by unwanted
Pounds,
Age ticks away the hands of a clock
The sand slowly falling
In the bottom of the glass
Covered over for the next generation to walk on
Maybe find maybe not
Trapped in this order and power
To the dreams of the future
And the game to concur
Waste

Road to Reflection

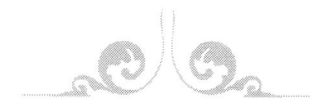

A Wish Then to Condition the Soul (part II.)

Of a breath
A simple moment
Wisdom from silent's and
then it's over,
Why live again if it leaves you unfulfilled?
Why take the path of hardship
When there is a way already explored
Easier to die than live,
But the fact remains
Can't accept failure
or being wrong
Want to be the best we can be
At everything
So much for hope,
A wish then to condition the soul...

James R. Saner II

Art of Remembering...

Slow dreaming, quick Wake
There was no mistake in her choosing
Pre-dawn glow, Shifting skies
Eastern horizon, Day-time
Night falling Westward
bringing magic and enchantment
Breeze of perception
Life dying
Children, Gangs; Like minded parades
Evolution on the course of achievement
Letting the mystery go on
Eating at the souls captor
One moment I was and then the next I wasn't
Strange, Better
Day's continue to add up
Nights passage forgotten
And then revisited
The new friend with old memories
Season of thinking
Art of Remembering...

Road to Reflection

"Thoughts of Reasons Floating in the Clouds."

Book of Russell
Preview

James R. Saner II

Book of Russell–I

The day time dreamer,
The traveler of tongues,
Named by Wontanamo the seeker.
Inspired by great men,
Old and ever aging souls.
A life's work, trapped in a single moment.
A dreamer's dream made into reality-The
Journey!
So many miles laid out in one small step.
The traveler gains courage and wonders into
A world he's just met.
Seeking accomplishments, looking for a
World known as Heaven!
He journeys onward,
Leaving home looking for God,
The almighty one.
Feeling the presence of the spirits &
Thanking them for their hands of guiding
Fortune.

Road to Reflection

Book of Russell – II

To gain the knowledge of reason,
To experience the senses.
To fully become aware of what it is to
Be human.
We watch it in different levels.
The truest feeling in us, still tucked
Away for safe keeping.
Ready, to be remembered.
Locked away is thought,
Reference for a better way of doing things.
The sky was once the limit.
Now it is space we are achieving.
No grief, to petty to morn for something.
To grown up, just by pass all those
Sentimental feelings—
Is what they taught!

James R. Saner II

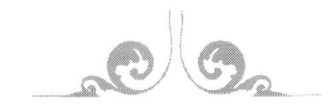

Book of Russell – III

He goes on a quest of ethics-Which religion
Is it?
He decides to forget it,
Starts his own writings and creates his own
Kind of faith.
His was independence! They followed.
The sheep who guided his shepherd.
Stuck in a life drama trying to avoid hell.
Here we are Hades. We are the devils
Separated from our glorious God & his
Glorious kingdom.
Outcasts, our soul thrown to the earth,
With a big bang we started. The process
Of growth, the ongoing development of
Aging. New levels of awareness,
New dimensions created.
Divided nations, states created, ways of
Life governmentally simulated.
Looking for an easier way of doing things.

Road to Reflection

Book of Russell – IV

Trying to find order in laws,
Instead of trying to find out what's right
Through feelings. Heart sunk deep, Best
Friends to the people you meet, Listening
And Understanding to what it is we all seek.
Questions like how long have I been asleep?
Or am I dreaming? The human curiosity!
When will I awake? Death games, we have
Died several times, Yet we've been reborn
Just as many. Who is the Christ and does he
Have the key to unlock this place? Buried
Deep down inside you.
Acceptance of fate-Destiny. Loving our
Creation is the only
Way of surviving. Eternal damnation that
Sounds great!
Sarcasm to our disgrace.

James R. Saner II

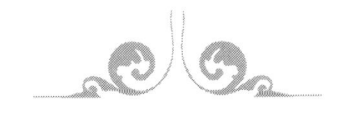

Book of Russell – V

Hope floating, lost in space-Save us!
Lend me your knowledge of life,
Produce the Father's love.
Last days are coming,
The one who comes to judge us.
The gift of reason
The ability to comprehend reason.
Chances drifting into supernatural
Situations, Undefined proclamation.
Unexplainable occurrence.
Satisfied my thirst.
Drank from the cup—Poisoned.
Death becomes us.

Book of Russell–VI

Angels, Spirits, Humans.
All messengers from the Holy one!
Are words not that powerful?
What is so different from these words?
Sounds pretty similar to the bible.
I'm also a servant,
Who speaks strait from the heart.
Forgiveness,
No one has figured it out
Or shared it with us.
Not as of yet.
they are coming-
Visitors from another planet
Public announcers,
Must find out whether or not
To fear these creatures.

James R. Saner II

Book of Russell – VII

I don't think they will travel here from
A far away land just to destroy us.
We are on the bottom of the Evolutionary
Ladder. No threat to space travelers.
We welcome them.
Night my friend is coming.
Interrupting the day's activities,
Throwing a little balance into the equation!
Day comes back again as the earth spins.
New dates and everything.
The new Messiah,
The new way of life,
The leader of the people arises!
Comes from the father or mother,
Depends on the religions description.

Road to Reflection

Book of Russell–VIII

Prophecies written—Fulfillment.
The Apocalypse!
Every knee shall bow,
Every tongue confess,
That the Lord is the Lord!
With no question they follow.
Miracles, Faith, Healed,
No more torture,
God is coming.
Let God come through you.
Speak through you.
But how they ask?
Trust your heart's judgment.
Feel what you must do as is written.
Humility through your actions.

James R. Saner II

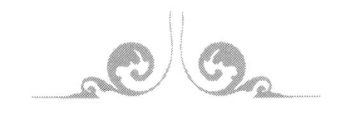

Book of Russell – IX

I don't mean to sound as if
I alone have all the answers.
I am trying to encourage my people to trust
Themselves. We can't entirely depend on
Another, We must learn our limits of our
Own independence.
The soul is a powerful force
That has been hidden from you by the
Rulers of the land and the churches.
People God is God!
No one can know It for you.
God is your friend.
You listen—Be patient
He/she will come to you. You'll realize
Always been present!
Seeming uncertain and unknowing
The future has not yet happened,
But is foretold.
You are the prophecies,
You really are that important.

Book of Russell – X

The relativity of good and evil.
Either for or against.
Choice of sides.
Which will I stand.
No force in your decision.
God if it were only that simple.
Right or wrong!
We have all been both
And we will continue to do so.
Listen to your own thoughts and understand
Your total feel for this world.
In the physical sense.
Humble thy self
In ones own self image,
Unworthy but forgiven.

James R. Saner II

Book of Russell – XI

You of age and of youth
Both my children and my parent.
We are of the same bloodline and Holy spirit.
Thankful for your existence.
So help me God, I will shine for you like
The sun of day, that blesses Mother Earth.
Captured by her truly magnificent beauty.
The worker who takes pride in his work and
The quality of his doings, is the one who
Knows the lessons of labor.
The worker which is God who works through
You as the laborer.
The true meaning of a Poet's words is the
Voice of God written and spoken.
With all that people know and All of their
Experiences shared and remembered,
We come to a point where God is Reflected-
A Mirror!

Road to Reflection

Book of Russell–XII

Honored by mine and your existence
The gathering of spirits.
We as a whole show the Magnificence and
Brilliance of the creator.
All Ideas have importance.
Ideas signify movement of time
Toward the future.
I haven't even begun to live,
This is only the beginning.
The second, third, and fourth coming
Of our savior.
These words I speak are also a part of
History.
Peace is the only way I'm afraid to do it.

James R. Saner II

Book of Russell–XIII

Expansion of our possessions.
We will sing in honor,
But we will also sing for the glorious
Sound, To hear and listen to it's
Marvelous message.
When we take into consideration all that
Is around us at any given moment is
God's image.
Shining through the images
Is God's self
Reflecting like a mirror to you.
Learn of the power,
See deep within and share your spirit with
Your friends.
Only you can save us!
Meaning Me!
Meaning You!
Meaning Us!
Meaning God!
Helping the world's population.

~To be continued~

Road to Reflection

Being Really

The good life of a man
Has no limits of wealth,
The bad means going to hell,
Well we see sometimes the
Way we choose is wrong
But the convention wow!
So small in time the heaven's
access blocked off no more entry
Live events stored away in
Anthology's keeping the secrets
of all the soon to be dead poets.
World bashed poetry
Mocked for being really
something of a cheap trick
Walking down the avenue
Waving a shoe licking her lips
Wanting something from all the
Famous poetry society's, The prize
Like we could be bought
Please this man is priceless...

James R. Saner II

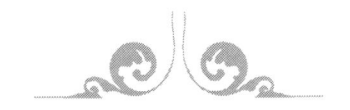

Best Part of The Day

When I was a child my Dad used to hold me in his arms when he got off work,
Hold me and rock me for hours
He told me later that coming home was the best part of his day,
He said when he'd see me and I always had a smile for him the world would go away and it would just be us,
He thanked me many times for my love
I thanked him for his as well.
My days aren't so far off from his
My children grow and I know the lesson my Dad gives.
May we all be so blessed.

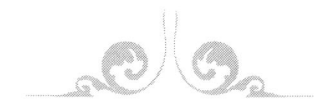

Blessed & Forever Blessing

Passion in a breath, life in a moment
taking it all in going and going
seeking truth and living a lie
staying within the white and yellow lines
grass is good to drive on
ticket only cost money
honey a little taste of
funny to be in this spinning motion
traveling in the light and in the darkness
White and black muddy waters
slave to a master only by choice
it is safer to accept then to achieve
stay in line please, order by control
it is harder not to believe in god
than it is to believe, come on do you really
feel that you are alone?
Faith in and so i become...
I know love (thank you so much) beyond words
Blessed & forever blessing.

James R. Saner II

Blessed Curse

Speak to me not with words But feelings,
Life eternal living never really stopped
Closer we come to the ever present now
We welcome you to the gathering
Souls unite giving form to the source
We came from, shape seen in the sphere
Strongest structure ever We become together
our maker "Center of the Universe"
Only ONE life force conclusion
Blessed curse of ours to say again and again
Curse of want Curse of need
Desire becomes both; Our understanding
Feel with me now FOREVER then
Feel with me now again and again
The rotation of this moment
This passage I saw the son was born and
reborn.. The night of his heritage,
Continuing on with the sharing of this
message, Look and see the Blessed
Are also the cursed Without connections...

Road to Reflection

Burned In My Mind

Give me Reason and I'll give you
Faith, The joining of;
Awakened my spirit Has moved on
In this realm of myth and of dream
Do you really see
What the future brings?
Like a queen she
walks with head held high
Carrying her cross Going to die,
Children gather and cry out
The Earth moved with magic
Braking the ground The sea
Shot forth and became;
I saw a single rotation
And the universe came
It went quick as it arrived.
But I saw it still,
Burned in my mind...

James R. Saner II

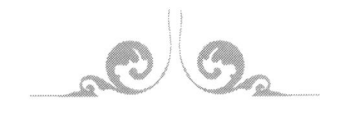

Changing of A Season

Forest of the dark wood
Enchanted dwelling, Native roots
Planted in the soft soil, Just enough light
to grow, Moss covered rocks
Creek bed shrinks and swells
Changing of a season
Cold to hot Blooded creatures
Harmony seekers Living in the wood
Wind whispers secrets of time
Before, Now
It is of age and yet still it grows
I ask you
How long do we have to live?
Changing of the watch hands,
Pretend that it is this time
Instead of that time
The things we change
The things we leave behind...

Circle of Elders I

One night in a dream,
I traveled to the land of the dead, So many
souls gathered in a village,
As I walked through the crowds
I was greeted by so many Who seemed pleased
that I was here, I continued on through the
heart of the people, Going to the council,
So many smiles and cheers as I past
standing bodies, Then the circle opened up
to me. The ancients let me sit
and have say in the council,
One elder spoke and the winds shifted
My brothers and sisters we must
give thanks to the Great Spirit who
Is and is not, We must give thanks for the
life we were allowed to live as human beings,
We must give thanks for the life we have
been given,
Today here in this place of dreams and
nightmares.

James R. Saner II

Circle of Elders II.

When the Elder was finished with his piece,
I spoke up
Where I come from the Order continues to
improve
People are losing the spirit in things
And have no guidance as to why they live
As children we are separated from our parents
By work
School
and other things,
The leaders of my world are continuing with
Wars and trying to hold what little power
They may have,
We as humans have lost our path and are lost
On a Dark road.
What light there is in my world is dim
and grows dimmer with the cycles of the moon,
Is there something that this council can do?

Road to Reflection

Circle of Elders III.

Another Elder spoke up, Ah young Sky Wolf it
is good to see you here in this place with
us, It is good to have you in this circle,
The ways of power are within you and you will
Know the power of such things when the time
is Right. Maintain and have faith,
For the world is but a reflection of bigger
things at work in the Universe,
Your world will be corrected in its Turn,
But know this young Sky Wolf you will help
bring the balance back and help the circle
find its completion again,
as it has been since the beginning so shall
it be at its End. Go now young one your time
here has past, I awoke from this dream
With a quiet knowing and Truth beyond my
understanding, calculate the number and come
to Wisdom, It is the way of our people to
grow in Knowledge...
May the Spirit be strong in you All!

James R. Saner II

Cloud Drifts

The cloud drifts above my head,
The strange song heard from a distance
Memories of a city cast in moonlight
Full Moon Rising Images for a life's
time burned into my mind to come again
into this Strange and wanting world
Giving Reason where there is none
Laughing at thoughts I should not be
thinking Then again I am- is gone
The sound is of sweet rhythm- ancient,
haunted, Lost but found
yet staying ever hidden
In the realm of enchantment,
do you hear the sound?
Feel the voice of wisdom
Feel the most amazing remembrance
Our journey's end, Life's completion
The cloud is overhead growing as we
Approach Death, It is to be
amazing...

Road to Reflection

Come To Life

Come to life,
This light I have inside me
Awake and be well the spell
I so desire to cast,
Mask the dark demons, Picked up by a caring
Father, Brother here to help,
Mother catching her children
In her wet sands, rock, and oceans
Come to life,
The spinning of the Heavens, A path leading
us back Home, We've been gone awhile,
Ancient wars and Elders, Sharing wisdom of how
to be eternal, Old souls reborn in a young
world, Of false order and Trust, Made to
believe in society
Come to life,
The depths of my being, Grow then be
Complete in this time, Fear not the making
Of our choosing,
Come to Life...

James R. Saner II

Creations End

When the walls breathe
And the ceiling dances
Trances through the dream
Awoken in a place
Full of faces looking
With expectations of creations end
Painted canvas
No white left visible
the images take form
Picture of a window
The doors closed shut
Locks being secured
Screams of some bodies
Then no more
Quietly the walls drew in a breathe
And the ceiling stopped dancing
Silence
The trance has gone....

Creator of Such Things & Created

In this I am
then I am not,
Just a name
Face
Body,
I am the spirit
Living breathing flesh
Saved in life and death
Creator of such things and created
I am connected to the source
In me there are many gifts
Talents to be given
Shared by the collective body of yours,
It is for you to accept
Be kind in the things you receive
In turn give as you have been given...

James R. Saner II

Creators Love

All in the creators love,
Of man and woman united bond
Sacred life sacred love
When you ask you shall receive
For it is in need that we believe,
It is this reason that we have come to know
It is seeing the truth in us all
Knowing instead of thinking
Doing instead of trying
Being who we are and reflecting
The creators love...

Down The Road

On the road, Wet dripping
Walking barefooted and the rains
still poring down, Shaking body
Waking mind Exploding with visions of native
charm and dancing
Freedom of the wakeful
Come again into the dream
Live forever and the music grows louder Now
Night has taken shape
The Road has ended
Cleansed by the movement of time
Legion Has gone back to the abyss
Walking off the cliff clinging to life
Like a child just born.
Breathe the gift, Whisper madness
Into the ears of the dying
As we set foot once again on the path
Of never more. As we become what it is
We were before. I picked up my boots
Turn and keep on walking back Down the Road.

James R. Saner II

Endless Dream

In the endless dream we wake,
In the timeless measure of-
We grow,
Play for me the moon
Again full lasting longer
Than before,
In the endless dream we wake,
Waves hit the shore
With force of creation's movement
Time died long ago,
In the endless dream
I find myself
Gone Lost in the world
The known,
In the endless dream (I'm home).

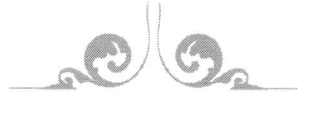

Eternal Living

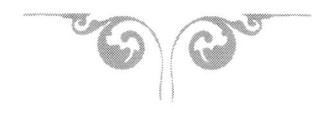

To tell the truth we must first know it,
Being in darkness some beings will never
Find it, Continuing to drift without light
Going deeper and deeper into the never
Ending nightmare of Hades, the lands of
the dead who don't know it, a mess of
Life's journal edited, erased from the
Forward moving life of eternal souls who
Grasp life and feel the calling of the
Creator to keep breathing, keep going,
We shall roll the rock up the mountain
Just to roll it back down again. Over
And Over until the rock is nothing more
Than a pebble, Learn to deal with the
Gifts you've been give, understand that
The creator is with you always, loves
you always, provides for you always,
Because we have the eternal life
We've been living and will continue to live.

James R. Saner II

Face in The Sky

After the dark
Spread its wealth
And the sun rested
I awoke
in predawn myth
Reflected the Spirits
Of this world to the next
And so forth
Rising in time to see
the clock face in the sky
Point me in the right direction,
Voyage to past life adventures
Wounds just freshly scabbed over
Picked at in the Night
Healing realized in this
dream of wakeful Wonder
Am I really what I perceive myself to be?

Road to Reflection

First Week

She has got to be the most
Wonderful woman in the world,
Sometimes
Other times she is the biggest
Witch,
That is my wife,
Holding stuff over my head
Saying things that hurt me
After all she was the one who
Chased after me now she is saying
She doesn't want me.
This is only after the first week
My god,
I need a shrink
Maybe some drugs and maybe a drink-
Death if it wants me
You may have me...

James R. Saner II

Freedom

The blood of Freedom shed,
The hurt of the people felt
But not dead,
We stand to fight
Not flee!
The blood of Freedom flows for you
As it flows for me,
We walk in honor
And are willing to die
for our Freedom.
Freedom is Freedom,
Let it be so,
But don't come here and think
That it is free
For there is a price for everything,
Blood is the price of our Freedom.

From Within

In the mirror
The reflections fade
Shape shifting into space
Taking form in backward direction
On the other side of the glass
Looking inward Familiar
Something new Yet seen many times before
Real truth I know not the face I see
Is it really me Ponder the question
It can't be
My face is the face I have not seen
My face is mystery to me
Parts of the body I can see
But not the face of my being
My eyes in the mirror intense
Light surrounding the body
It shifts again
And I look within
The familiar stranger
I saw from within…

James R. Saner II

Frost

Listen to me the wind
speaking softly says
I will change the season
Give the warmth to the other side of the
World
You will receive the cold dark winter
And suffer through the night
Chilled to the very bone
I shall not come again
Lost in the dark mist of morning
The birds song shall not hit your ears
You have been cast into eternal darkness
Open your eyes,
Breath deep my frost.

Full Volume

We feel the dance in us,
Trance in us
Songs screamed out by us,
Life concurred death in this mess
We confess we helped build in us
Allowed the piano to be left
Guitar strings to be broken
Houses to be run down in us
We rebuild in us
filled in us
Turned up the Music
FULL VOLUME in US
We screamed at Death
And he just left
Went to go get this ODE!!!

James R. Saner II

Gentle Reflection

Gentle reflection,
I stand before the mirror
What is behind me I feel but will never see
A spirit, holy ghost, energy
I see my hands
My arms,
My chest
My legs
My feet,
But I will never be able to see me
Completely.
Gentle reflection,
The image in this mirror
Isn't me.
But I accept him
As myself,
My Body...

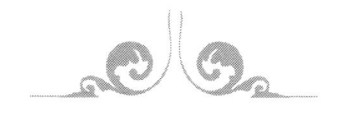

Good Man Passing

As the light grew near
Mothers screams were heard as I was
passing through the womb
She held me as I bleed into her
saying you're a good man my little son,
As I age my life has stages
Shows and musicals
Laughter mixed with pain
Blood spilled tears
Working hard for my own little ones,
As the light fades and my hair grays
children having their own lives
And dramas
My last breath flooded with Death
Fever guides me home.
As I leave I finally see the Truth
She whispers good Man passing...

James R. Saner II

Great Cycle

In the time after this,
When all is found and in the process of
Understanding
I will already be gone, Missing
You will try to feel the things that I have
Felt,
You will try to find my understanding
The meaning in the words
A story of past to present and then to future
Some will tell you what they think I meant
And others will find new meanings,
Be one of these for then you will find the
Vision, the truth of our beings
For it is in living that I have found my
Death and it is in Death
That I shall begin to live
The great cycle
The Sphere is in motion
And the motion is constantly Aging...

Road to Reflection

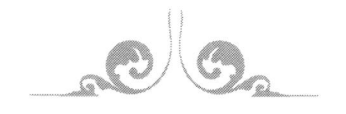

Greatest Of These

If I could see your face again,
If I could walk across the winds,
I would,
Believe it,
If I could kiss your lips again,
If I could climb the highest mountain
Fly up to the moon
I would,
Believe it,
Faith, hope, and love they are divine
Faith she's just a stranger,
Wanting to tempt me into trust,
Hope I don't believe her
But the Greatest of these is Love
If I could cure the Disease
If I could give you back your life
I would,
Believe it,
Faith, hope, and love they are divine
And the Greatest of these is love

James R. Saner II

Guide Me Love

There is a wedge between us
That is my
Self
Fear of purpose
And what I must do
Fear of failure
Fear of Truth
I am nothing without you,
So close to the Source
Still a ways to go,
Becoming
Growing,
I accept your truth,
I will Do
I Will do,
Thank you for your Peace
And Light
I am as you are!
Guide me Love...

Hall of Echoes

A message has arrived no equals
Have a sign the ones who walk with you
Take their own path sometime.
Change is the same game
Native pride want nothing be nothing
Freedom has enslaved me
Chasing my tail for a time
Like a dog
young pup out in the yard laying in the grass panting,
Hall of Echoes
The dance of my voice
Quieted by the distance of this chamber
Even the most wise
Are fools sometimes…

James R. Saner II

He Just Left...

Enough I say of twisted tongue confusion
Rambling man take a stand and battle
The bands illusion,
A great thing to mock the Gods
A mistake to think all falls on Deaf ears
For I hear you and you do not sound like the
One I sent before you, No snake to ride
I am afraid
The bus will do you better,
The ship whistles its final call
To the ones not yet aboard,
Come one come all to the last great
Sound,
It is alive and dying
All in a single breath
The magic of the ages changing faces
He just Left....

Road to Reflection

Heaven in Your Smile

I give you Heaven in my smile
Heaven in my smile
With my touch I'll set you free,
Because baby I love you to much maybe
You're all I'll ever need.
I give you Heaven in my smile
Heaven in my smile
With my kiss I'll set you free,
Because baby I love you too much maybe
You're all I'll ever need,
My Angel child,
You give me Heaven in your smile
Heaven in your smile,
The gift I give you give to me,
You're all I'll ever need....

James R. Saner II

Hello Moon

Hello trees
Hello stars
Hello moon
Hello trees
Hello stars
Hello moon
Where are you, where are you
I'm coming too
Hello trees
Hello stars
Hello moon
In the evening we sit and commune
Hello trees
Hello stars
Hello moon

Road to Reflection

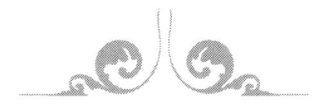

Hells Edge & Heavens Gate

What if I found the Dawn Caused the moon to
Show its other-side Would I then be worth it?
What if I said I could do it
Would you wait to find out or run then slow
down looking back for a single moment
Seeing the place where we once stood
together, What if I could pin point the
disease and cure it Would I then be worth it?
Hope Light on the brink of Brilliance
Fading away in Darkness Not enough fuel
to feed the fire the flame died...
The Man's imperfect Number
Caught in a slumber of sleeping
Gods distaste for its kind
Flawed by the serpent's temptation
Thought it all away,
Couldn't bare to live another day
In this make shift reality of
Hells edge and Heavens gate,
The wars End...

James R. Saner II

Here

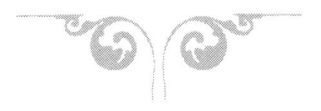

Then
Again
I find it here
Distance
Across the seas,
Population
One Nation
Circle of stars appear
Gaps
Between
The people,
Main land
Which one?
Here...

Holiday

When God takes a holiday,
Where does that leave us?
Who is in charge?
Forget the world and what it teaches you
Find the one true source
That makes you.
The light in whose image we reflect.
I Know This Form,
This way of being.
Light and darkness battle for time daily.
Night and Morning forming forever,
The being we label as Omega.
This battle is the way,
This is the truth
We have it in us to stop the world,
Only we label it Death as Alpha,
The Beginning verses The End of our reality.

James R. Saner II

In Some Ways

The prayer is heard
Last chance,
Last dance
Holy ghost smoken'
Joes camel burned
Down to the butt.
A way to stay true
Is to die a thousand times over
Then go for a dip in the pool.
Make shift reality
Visions of the lost world-
TRUTH...

Road to Reflection

Fiction Shares

The image of what's real
Sometimes
gives you a break
From your world-
Pause then quotation
Alpha
Omega
Letters symbolize
Communication
So far off in it,
Trippin'
In the fields
Crossing the rivers
Swollen...

James R. Saner II

For My Son

He dream's still good
Go and do what you want to do,
What needs to be done
Do it.
Live as yourself
Never forgotten
Love is a blessing
You are blessed
Grow with the spirit
And stand silent for in the
Quiet you will find knowing
Save the last words for
The ones who will listen
Share the message of God.

If You Had

If you had the time would you share
With me.
If you had the time would you share
With me.
Happy together we will always be..
If you had the time would you share
With me.
If you had the time would you share
With me.
Forever together anyway
Forever together anyway
If you had the time would you share
With me.
If you had the time would you share
With me.
Through heaven we go-
Just so you know, forever together
You and me.
If you had the time would you share
With me.

James R. Saner II

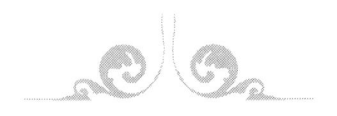

Imagine The Dreamer

When the Moon passes the sun,
The day comes back again.
The story is not false or fiction
But simple Truths laid upon the Heart.
Are we strong enough to seek these simple treasures
to see the sun's insight of the moon
blocking it's brilliance,
We should be able to reach up and grab the moon
But then again what of distance.
Undo the lesson
Imagine the dreamer
Who dreams this world into existence
A part of but not really
For they are the matter and we are the form.
A Greater body so to speak,
What is greater than me?
You?
We?
Us? All in the same being...

Road to Reflection

In Another Life (part I.)

Yet to speak with the gift of voice,
no one has heard the depth of my sound
A scream in the moonlight
Lifted over the chilling winds
the call travels beyond the worlds
Rise up ye who have grown cold and still
over time and have waited for thy breath
to be given yet again a chance to live
Maybe this time forever
Blood in the moon the moment has come
We gather for purpose and the dance
Wolf take care to speak and lead this circle
The twists and turns
The long dark snake
Roads we walk on
The roads they paved

James R. Saner II

In Another Life (part II.)

Lead me not into the quiet mind
Let me meet with the king and queen
so that I might enter her still
And give the king his ransom
Shall I knock quietly at thy door
Fear has enabled he to answer
A shout on the other side of his door
Guards take him away.
Laughter in my madness
I take my chains back down the hall
The Guards pass me by as I whisper
in their ears
Maybe in another life...

In Another Time

String of thought,
the never world
Words lost—spoken in another time
Mind if I show you
The door of existence
Walking blindly forward
Into a light so vast and taking
We come to the next me
Neighbor
Good to see everything so tasteful
Going well,
I saw myself There then Here
Over and Over
Spinning entranced
The dance of a madman
Chant of a shaman
Circle of magic
Spells of medicine
The Cure...

James R. Saner II

In Life In Death

The need arises, but is it met?
No matter how hard we try there is
No guaranty of success, The faithful who
Turned into our betrayal,
Wishes of greater happenings
Dream seekers who weep for the future,
She Bled...
I drank the blood,
But never tasted the flesh.
Sacred stones placed in time we
Never met,
Left here Now so filled yet so empty
Calling on the God for release,
Let go please
Let me rest
In Life In Death

Into The Dream

And we drift into the dream,
We float down the river,
And we drift into the fall
The earth still spinning
The sun comes up
The sun goes down
The earth still spins and like a clown
I wonder why I'm here
Do you see my tears?
Do you see my eyes?
Take away my pain
Take away my struggled life,
And I know that I'm alone
And I know that I am home
But I still don't know
And we Drift into the dream....

James R. Saner II

Invasion

Balance
Foresight visions
The Red Dragon
Masses
Wave of human beings
Awaking from a dream
To many
Silence is deafening
Screams cut like a knife
The air
Burning buildings
Crumbled
Death rage
War
When it happens
Will you fight
or be no more?

Road to Reflection

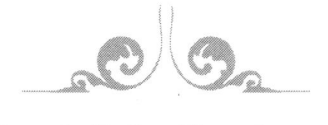

Invisible Society!

Invisible Society!
The moth on the wall
The ghost in the hall,
They seem to be hiding something.
Protecting an object,
Securing safety for the individual!
Strangers
Members to an invisible society,
Nurturing a child
Guiding life's process,
Not to quick to interfere,
They have been labeled angels,
But really they are Holy Spirits.
Divine messengers
Our worlds savior
By faith alone will they appear.

James R. Saner II

Just fall

Rivers of passion
Gentle touch of love
So close to Heaven
Just fall
Away we go
Losing center
Focus
Lost control
in the grove of
Molded in another's love
Energy, tingles~
You and I both
Communication
Destination
To bed we go...

Road to Reflection

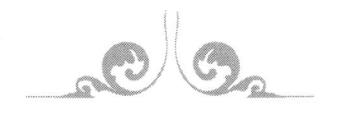

Keep on Living

How many of us do you need?
Is our labor worthy of your Prophet?
It's a make shift dream
Reality of one Master to another,
How many lives created for this purpose?
Can Death keep up with the process?
When I awake and see the Truth of my efforts
will I be proud or will I crumble in my own
Stupidity? Civil war
Divided nation
Power play with the peoples choice,
And if I don't choose
What then?
Or if I never awake,
Just continue on in this dream until
the day breaks,
What then?
Some questions are never answered
And some we already know the answers to,
Thus we keep on living...

James R. Saner II

Knowing It Is So

Feel without feeling
Love without loving
Hope without hoping
Faith in the unknown
Knowing it is so
Doing without trying
Seeking instead of waiting
Focusing instead of thinking for it is a
waste of energy,
The great quest
Challenge
Forgive them, they know not what they do.
Acting instead of talking
Waking instead of sleeping
Being who you are instead of questioning
Always becoming more....

Road to Reflection

Leader

Dance with me spirit of day
Into the other world of morning
Place of endless space
Case thrown out of the court room
Faceless nameless lost ones
Become two three and four
For pleasure and For pain
Game played with rules of
Unspoken creation,
Came about some way other than
By time talent took hold of the
Gifted creator being god me someone
Chosen for the leader.

James R. Saner II

Least of These

I am their Dad,
I am here to help them grow and learn
Give them Love,
Give them tools to craft in this world.
If only I could live up to the image
I am in their eyes, My God that would be
Humbling, All life is Holy
For the battle of the ages, there must be an
End now. So Bring it on then
You Legion of Demons
Bring on your Holy war and
see the rivers of blood
pool in the after math and process of,
Freedom has no limit,
It cannot be stopped,
For it is the wheel that keeps on rolling,
Beyond Death
And Beyond Life…
It is the nature of things.

Road to Reflection

Liberty for All Mankind

As she enters the town in her Force,
The enemy fleeing,
As she stands tall and just
The earth rumbles
Her Army of One
One soul
One nation
One being
Connected in life
Rapped in Freedom by her Banner
Her torch raised high and Burning
Let my people be Free she is heard screaming
Rise up and take light in my flame
For you are my people and I
Your Bride,
Liberty for all mankind...

James R. Saner II

Life Work

I want to try the things I haven't
Let me see the world in its true self
Give me peace to live my life
Let me be some help.
Life works filled in with a pen,
do you remember me as I am,
Did you believe you could win?
For a moment I thought you were some
one else.
But you're still you and I'm still me.
We shall soon grow into someone we both
will never know as our self
This art of aging makes me crazy.
The last line makes no sense…

Little Voices

Little voices born to the world
To learn to speak and sing
Little bodies enter through the womb
Blood covered bodies,
Slapped they scream
The first sound they make
Music in the way of our beings
A vibration that shakes the heavens
And brings a smile to the creators face
Little people they become as they age
Living to become someone great
Growing into the Great I am
They then become MEs
And a part of WEs forming a greater song
These little voices are ours
And we are theirs
The collective body of together
Being Family
Like father, mother
Son and Daughter; All the little Children...

James R. Saner II

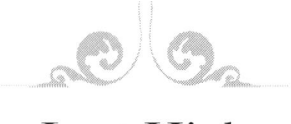

Lost High

I've lost my High,
I have forgotten what it is to be free
from all this,
In my youth I found freedom in the smoke,
but then I took a drink and grew old
I could find my high with an open heart
take a trip into the hills and get lost,
I could sit for hours and have peace
writing it all down for whoever to read
No fear of aging know thoughts of defeat,
I was immortal here and gone all in the
same moment, Constant in my being
I was the god whose name you knew not
but the being you could feel when you just
stopped, I was the power of mystery
I was the drug to cure disease,
I was the chosen one the great I am
and then I was just me, I could give
you comfort and bring you peace, I was so
close, that you could almost see...

Lucky Ones

Slow is the death I wish to hold,
Sharp is the pain that I do carry,
Bright is the light shining in my eyes
The spark of magic and then there's real life
I struggle to maintain in this fragile
Reality of control and breaking order,
Desert sands no running water
Thirst for a drink of insight
Money a thing that comes and goes
To quickly, to many Masters wanting
My things, nothing but words to many
To fill me up inside with stress
And the day to day things, no time for
Sickness or rest, just keep on going
Giving and giving. What happens when I can
Give no more? Will I be finished
Just rushed out the door? Other mouths
To feed and then to think that we are the
Lucky ones with opportunities to achieve,
Selfish to me the things I see.

James R. Saner II

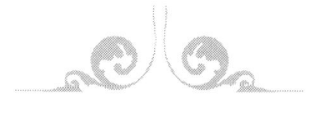

Master

Touched by the love entangled by the emotion
Flood of passion Clouded perception
Tripped over the rug As I entered the house
Great is thy chambers Dwelling on the hill
side Manners to good not to Allow entrance
You have bid your share of work
And labored your fare share of wages
I commend you to become free, grant you
Pardon No more slavery to this master,
The master says go I give you, your life
Then I shall be the master and you the slave
Earn your freedom or enter the grave
Hosted parties of lust & disease
I fluster in my freedom in wrong choices
Lack the vision of opportunities
Decision so simple and becoming
Harder to make I blew it all away,
Enslaved by my Freedom My Freedoms master
My Freedoms slave I chose the grave,
Didn't see the new Master coming.

Road to Reflection

Matters and The Body

Walking the path less chosen
Becoming more
Leaving what is less than
Better way of living
Choice not really
Questions that need not be answered
Yet the search to do so
The middle grounds
Matters and the body
Light in the center
Earth shaking sound
The voice of man
the eyes of the Wolf
Power in the silence of Knowing
In the shadow
Behind you it is there
Your own...

James R. Saner II

Me and Mine

Wishes never coming true,
Cries of a child not being heard
Forgetting what is real and going into
Our minds twisted game of what ifs
And it could happens, Just like my
Wish of being known for something great
Such as the writings we gave,
Future might be the only way of letting
Me be known, I am afraid I will not
Be here then, Plagued by my stupid thought
If it could stop and let me be for just
One moment maybe I could forget this
Wish of mine and find something else
To try and take me into the silence of our
Minds
No more games
No more time
Life forgot Me and Mine....

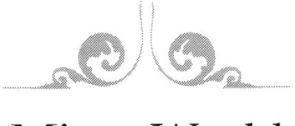

Micro World

Make sure to leave your feelings at
The door, come inside and see logic
Take control, funny it is when you
Never enter because of fear our failure,
So close to knowing we find ourselves
Still just out of reach of achieving
The things we wish to know,
Like how on Earth am I so-
So what that's what I want to know
What in the world am I?
Just a definition or stream of energy
Creating a micro world out of remembrance
Or experience of mankind a millennium ago
I am no God but let me Know God so that
I might just be saved from this scriptural
Life.
No Death for me this time. No Life!!!

James R. Saner II

Mission

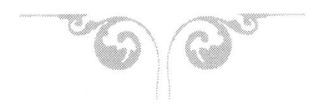

Did I ever tell you about the time
Beyond beginning
Or how the whole thing began?
Well let me tell you about Mission
Down in the heart land,
Grand stand center stage shared the
Whole thing live on radio,
Gathering crowds to spend the day
watching pig races and pie eating contests.
Well let me tell you about the Mission,
Which was for the savage natives, to
Tame and civilize there creation,
cut their hair and change their clothes
To something more tasteful, something
More Christian. Only then where they
Allowed to be sent to the reservation,
Giving the white man the proud City of
Mission. The little town I live in,
Ancient ghost wisdom fills the mist
In The morning just as the sun comes up.

Road to Reflection

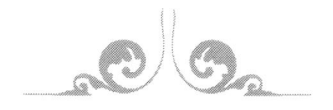

More Than Asked For

Reserve the right for another day,
You may need to change
List the subjects for...
Stored someplace in my dome
Home is
Like I say
Some way or where out here
Stoned
By people blind to faith
History in the making
Silly songs dusk till dawn
Every day is a today but before
It was tomorrow, Hence come again
That was yesterdays subject matter
I'm just
Need I say more
I can man
You know this because
Clear visions of salvations army
Giving the poor more than they asked for.

James R. Saner II

Music of Colors

Into the abyss
The tangled web,
Clouded heaven
Colors, wonders
enough said
Filled the hole with dirt
Black whole lot of colors here
Compressed
Stressed to the point of breaking,
I gave life to voice
Music of colors
Choose to either speak
Or be quiet...
words were written
Before they became song
Music of Colors
Blood was Red
I hear the hummmmmmmmmmmmmmmm~~~

Road to Reflection

My All

Is my Temple worthy of you oh spirit,
Am I giving it the shape you so choose,
Live in side this temple Oh great spirit
May my body be thine own
Dance in the circle spirit
Breathe life into these bones
Make me part of the One great spirit
I wish it to be so
Let the Mystery take shape oh spirit
Let your divine presence be known
Thank you for the gift great spirit
Show me what it's for
Let me be thine apostle
Reborn or born again
I am here now let it be so
Into your love oh spirit
Into your home
Take refuge in this temple
Spirit I will give you my all...

James R. Saner II

My Dept

I know not who he was talking to,
Only that he was talking,
My dept was paid
With my death
I then join the living,
Walking in the dreams
Tripped the hills
And saw many things
The poet and the pen
To many keys,
Typed in Plugged into the network
The fountain of existing known knowledge
We can find anything or anyone.
It stands true and shining
The tree did speak
But to who it seems mystery
I can say I listen
but do I hear,
For my riches have disappeared...

My Path

Looking back over the shoulder
Of my life I find a path,
My path, the way I chose to go
Then my gaze moves ahead
To where it is I'm going.
Steps before me steps behind me
Bothered by the distance of my journey
Dragging my feet slowing as I
Come to the next landing
Only for a moment I stop
First breathing
Then keeping in mind it's still a long
Way to go,
But when I get there,
Yes when I finally reach my goal
That is when I rest—I'm finally done.

James R. Saner II

Mystery

As I begin again today, A new life
Giving of this day Love to all
Love be with you in your wake
May the spirit of life and death
Be kind to you this day, Night in the
making forever rotating, Motion of the ages
Moon full and yet shadowed by our great light
Giving and taking as is only right
For in this battle of wills
And Fair trade, We see a balance of plus/minus
May the sum be equal and the Energy levels
rise, May you be complete in yourself
Reflect upon all things
And may all things treat you right
Grow as the tree only knows so well
May you be free and yet still have strong
roots, For there is no limit but the one
great Truth, Mystery, No one has figured it out...

Road to Reflection

Nights Passage

Dreaming child
nights passage
has claimed you, the open door
Morning rises when the sky is
rich with color Divided
To the West- The moon in all its glory
And to the East-The sun in all its power
Walk the balanced path
Into the space between
The worlds
The crow sat on the fence post
Watching Waiting
For the time to end
So that it could claim its victim
Feast on the soul of man
Black bird, Take what is yours
As Death passes bringing
nourishment to Life.
And so the cycle is completed
The child awoke enchanted...

James R. Saner II

No End to the Beginning..

From the skies I fly Through the breath of yours, On the ground I stand planted, deep are the roots of my life source, Dance the circle, Trance the flame be one, come again into the light of day, See the shift in
night continued, Sleep no more for the wakeful are watching, Screaming babies bring up the sun, Clouds forming, Rains Falling, Thunder whispers on the horizon, Trains and High ways, Constant madness for those who are lost in the maze, I see the pattern
Yet can't quite grasp the pen to recreate
the sadness into something new, Have I lost the way through? Just one more smoke before I close my eyes and enter the dream,
Let it be the road less taken,
Let it lead me home...
No end to the beginning...

Road to Reflection

No False Pretence

Fiction rings the bells of Truth
When searched for there,
Closed doors of imaginations locked
in the mind of the not knowing persons
Left with grief and remorse for
Uncertainties they had no clues of
Let us confess and repent for
Salvation from death or separation
Of the most high and knowing
If and only when we are willing
To be receive shall we then be
Delivered.
When seeking Truth be prepared
To accept it for when it comes
It comes with no false pretence,
But only as itself real as needed.
But rest assured it is never
More than a person can handle.

James R. Saner II

No Way Out of The Circle

What of this
To be set free in the halls of Liberty
The building blocks of Freedom
Stacked way up against me
Price of it all
Was infinitely expensive,
It cost me my soul
They come to collect soon
my pen just ran out of ink...
200 years gone
But here I am
Again and again
No way out of the circle
That's spinning,
What past life?
Can it be I just awoke
into the light of day
And Yet I still feel
the chill of the nights
claws releasing me from its grip...

Road to Reflection

Of Gods and Men

Of Gods and men
The great epic battles for glory and Honor
Horror and chaos, Right and wrong; All about
POWER, to taste the control have order
At your finger tips, To be served instead
Of serving, Of Slaves and Masters FEAR in the
Back ground haunting the mansion,
Of Guests and Hosts wanting the reservation
Welcome to the party, the so called Order
Of States and Nations conquest to grow
And become Greater,
Of the rich and the poor to open doors you
Must first have the keys,
Of Wisdom and Understanding we know not
But pretend we do,
Of Thinking and Knowing which is better
or is there such a thing?
Of Simple and difficult which is harder?
You might be surprised by the struggle...

James R. Saner II

Of My Own Perception

Other times it does remember,
That is why I'm comfortable.
Sitting in a restaurant
I am now reflecting back on
The occurrence of last nights wonder.
I borrowed the mike of the performer
And asked the audience for their permission
So that I might read one poem.
Few listened.
But I thanked them for their
attention and soon after I left.
The man said I didn't look like a poet.
I asked him what one looked like,
He didn't know!
I also thanked them for their applause.
That was warmth to my heart.
Lifted my spirit and Touched my imagination.

OLD As The Time Goes

Years stacked up with collections,
Writings not so valued
Lost in the mind was the student
Who grew into the teacher,
Yet had learned nothing to teach.
So maybe in a way it works for the better
Still hanging in the shadows of memory
trying to think off self doubt.
Fighting to stay focused on the coming
Days. The wars with our fellow nations
Starvation of the political camera
Leaders with death in their pockets,
For so many years now the dream has
Guided me to where I am now,
My own house, my own car, my own cat,
My own dog, and so goes the wife.
In the blink of my eye years have piled
Up, no room to be any more. Youth
Grown up so there you have it OLD as the
Time goes!

James R. Saner II

Old Troubled Strength

Worrying about things,
Simple petty things
Makes ya wonder about things
February days going my way
Over the bridge not coming back again
Years on a calendar
Pass you by with little recognition
of aging
Makes me crazy to realize
My youth is in a movement of growing
Wild
Maybe now my life will fly by
So much for learning reasons of why
Or who then, What now
My god
Willing or not it shall be ready
Major Life events
Tales of old troubled strength

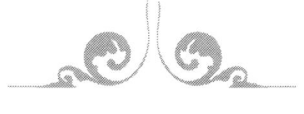

One Form

Imagery contained Fear
Which gives us hope of new creation,
Soul solitude,
When Death comes, Floats
going back from which it came-
By Fear and Trust
Faith over comes
Bringing new breath to a being
Which manifests from collections
Of words, thoughts, energies
Of The Dead
Find new Life in One Form.

James R. Saner II

One Soul

Before the beginning there was only One
Soul, One massive being; Cold, dark, and Lonely
I know this because I have seen it with
My own eyes and felt it with my own Heart
It is a quiet Truth that each of us knows,
In this being was great awareness and powerful
Knowing. (I have nothing and no one)
So I shall create It and Them; I will be
The Creator, The darkness created light
And the Cold became Warmer these things
Are simple to understand, In light
There are colors and in Warmth there are
Feelings, but to have another to share
It with is somewhat complex, So One
Started multiplying and creating itself a new
And itself it would recognize as You
A spirit a new being What we call Living,
Out of Awareness the equation grew and once
In motion it can never stop for there
Is Truly only One Soul, Whose I don't know.

Our Energies

Soft gentle kiss of the wind on
your neck feeling the mind connect
and rest with the soft gentle hand of god
knowing you, loving what it is you are.
Death in a single whisper takes you back
into the what we call normal
Hello is there someone here, lots of
times they answer yes yet this time
something's different,
Strange I never knew I looked like him
before...
Now you will see with his eyes all the
faith filled lies containing this world
in a single image to be damned
or better said kept unknowing to the
truth of our lives our energies...

James R. Saner II

Out Here Lost

Participating in the act
Movement on the stage
Becoming the character
And losing yourself
Forever we will be in this seen
My eyes are cloudy what was that
Thing falling
Luck of the draw minister of music
Soul pollution Devils
Up on the hill twisting figure
Distilled and blessed
Holy one on the mound going to
Strike out the last homerun hitter.
Ramblings missed factor configurement
Left to come on alone in the deep
Dark night. Come to fight
come to dine we will struggle one
More time but then it is over
Lost, Lost
Out here lost.

Road to Reflection

Plague of Souls

Act now,
Hope for praise later
May the lion
Protect the lamb
From the wolf,
But let the wolf have
His fill from the fallen
All about sin
The plague of
souls cleansed
After the light
Touches it.

James R. Saner II

Pre-dawn Glimpse

And now I come again into this quiet garden,
Wading through the words
Piled high like manure
Fertilized minds collide
Rebirth to the sleeping flowers
The bulbs lost their light,
How long must we be in darkness
Sunrise tides, heat brings smiles
Good morning to you,
Growth of a new form
Aging process of organic beings
I found my mortal soul singing for death's peace.
And now I come again into this darkness,
The sparks have faded and spring has not yet arrived,
Pre-dawn glimpse of what is coming...

Quick

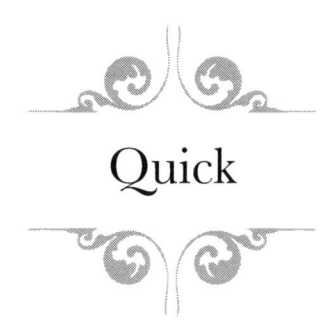

To soon for you wanting everything to be now
What is the problem with this fool thing?
Cut the crap jack and put it all back
Quick
Before they come through the door,
Time flies when you step with the quickness
To get it all done as best you can
Quick
Get the hell out before they take you to the moon
Back side, fun ride but not the anal probe
Silly old humans living in a shoe
Fantasy world of art and live news.
Wow, what's his face looks like his face is
glued to his skull, you know the senator from
Arizona, the republican, damn alien
Who does he think he's fooling?
Quick With milk is gooooood!

James R. Saner II

Quiet Mind

Honor of choice
Voice whispering madness
Sadness grips my bones
Alone,
Not so lonely
Eternal wind
Breathing life into my soul
A song of talent
Wasted on deaf ears
New challenges for a generation
Behind me
I leave my mark,
Come and find me...
I will share with you my secrets
Give healing to the sick body
Change the tides
By calling the moon
I will help save you
But only if you choose,
All in a quiet mind...

Read ON!

I am here for all to find,
I have been given unto you for my spirit
The living God inside of us
Before the day is through we
Shall know such love
We shall see such things as the
Motion of the sun burns up,
In the constant cycle of change
We grow and continue to become
We know wrong so we can know right
It is just to have a creator scorn us
It is beautiful to hurt so we may
Know how to heal,
It is good to be hated so that
We know how to truly love,
It is for us to give to others
And lead them home.
I know not the message in the words
Unless I read them for myself... Read ON!

James R. Saner II

Real for a Change (part I.)

I am no prophet,
Have nothing but imagination to conjure up
these things
No gods to worship but one
No Devils to fear
Just what I have been taught by others,
A History I have no way of proving
Only facts that have substance
Such as the sun rising
And then the night appears
I work hard to support a family
And my reward paper
I have been taught to value a system.
(Trade)My work has substance
And I can see the benefits to each project I am
A part of, I play a role as director
Designing nice things in peoples homes
Helping with the Cleansing of the body
Making sure that the showers shine
And the kitchens welcome you home,

Road to Reflection

Real for a Change (part II.)

There is passion in what I do
And there is much knowledge to be gained,
When you see others and there private spaces
You get a sense of Life
And a purpose to improve that Life
I am no salesmen for that is cold and empty
But I do provide service
with a smile and blessing
I am not rich in paper value or even well off
But my Trade provides me with what I need
And the knowledge of more to come.
Don't forget that the rivers provide us water,
That the earth provides our energy,
That even though we try to escape in doors
we still are here in this world.
I have no idea why I write this now
or even what it means,
Maybe it is peace of mind
Or maybe it is being real for a change...

James R. Saner II

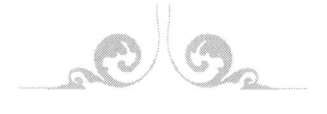

Reflect

Reflections of a growing consciousness
I can feel your eyes reading my words,
And I thank you for it,
The positive energy you share as the
More of you there are reading and knowing
My words are powerful,
Self reflection of a waking God,
We are all a part of the body
In turn our spirit dances on the wind,
Growing and gaining more from within,
Yet somehow through an outside source,
The connection is eternal,
Reflect with me bounce that energy Know
You believe and Be with me in everything,
You're all are a part of the one source,
Feel with me the consciousness, My
Energy is yours, God thanked the man
And he then created Woman. Or is it
The other way around. Both are important.
Reflect....

Road to Reflection

Regression to the Beginning

Ramblings, Pointless words
Regression, Obsession
Lost thoughts, spinning wheels
Traveling without even leaving my chair
Forgetting to remember
Dazed Glazed vision
Mind wandering out there
Perimeter
Thinking stoned images
Burned into my mind
The Cross
Roads meeting in the middle of
Without the lines
Unsure of where they lead
This way
That way
The End...
Ah Hell that lines been said many times
mind gone mad
The beginning...

James R. Saner II

Right Kind of Freedom

Under the moon The seas rise and fall Depth becomes deeper In the nights realm The passage of time stands still Opening the gate to Freedom Raging currents tides high to low Ride of a life time On and on this dream continues The rotations constant cycle The same fast speed Light and dark Caught in this balance Battle of wills A Draw: The Pawn has moved as far as it can go The witch was taken by the knight I took his with my Bishop Take the message for what it's worth Two powers struggle for advantage Is there such a thing To gain, have more of At what cost Worth more alive than dead Just words man From a leaky pen and in the events to follow Cleaning up this god darn mess Left by others for us to ponder Lose the ego Pride Self worth The image was just an image Caged animal Invisible chains Not the right kind of Freedom…

Road to Reflection

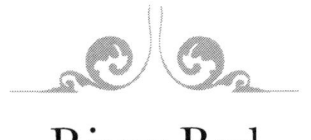

River Bed

Current takes me down river,
Floating on the tides of thought & wonder
Realizing this river flows through my house
Without this River I am unwashed
Left in the Mothers dust so to speak without
A tongue to praise or curse her
From this river bed I dream
See many things inside this image of
imagination
The illusion of the World
My character in this play of sorts
I seek the Truth behind the illusion
No more magic no more tricks
Just what is,
A Future...
Children laughing and smiling
Some are still sleeping
Take a drink of this...

James R. Saner II

Save US!

Lost in the emotion,
Finding commotion
Praying there will be a way
To save us,
Lord
Save us,
Save the world
Save the woman from her own inner battle,
Only one shall rule,
Save us Lord
Save us.

Secret Garden

Secret Garden
A rose growing in the cracks of the pavement,
Dreamers
Walking the path of Yesterday
To achieve the vision
tomorrow brings
Light danced its way through
the gardens maze
Fountains
long since flowing
Grown over with ivy
Secret garden
Our choice
Today
The gardener lay sleeping in the shrubs....

James R. Saner II

Shift in Season

Amazing day of peace, Filled up with spirit power, In the being of our remembrance Start the dance around the circle, Trance the magic sun, Moon glows Shadow of the Earth, Blanket for our peoples Warmth from a fire burning, Vision comes to our young ones, boys and girls Don't let the power see you wanting, For the gift is something that will be forever more. Need is of shelter, food, warmth for a hairless body, Animals who remove themselves from there nature, We eat and Crap just the same, Designer clothes and the best of taste, Animal something to be said about our being A part of the Earth and sky, We try to hide ourselves from what we are; The spirit of the Creator, Shift in season, Allow the knowing to be within you, Walk the road to becoming, Awake in a dream unknown The Power that walks with you Must be acknowledged

Road to Reflection

Sky

We laughed and sang songs, till the day
Went to long and then next day's sun
Was rising, fires in the sky twinkle
In her eye she went on dancing,
Rock me gently hold me tight kiss me
One more time, don't leave me yet
We just met come with me tonight,
Not to far now we're almost there
Someplace we called home, Lost the
Way there don't be scared just keep
Sing'n your song, another time she
Does remember when the rains fell
From the sky, let it go now walk
On down the road now leave us
To our night, We laughed and sang songs,
Till the day went to long and then
The sun fell from the skies.

Spinning No More

Light body
Levels of colors
Vibration new form
Reason in the clouds
Floating
Lost out here on the edge
Mind playing with magic
Waking the dead
The river of thought
Time stopped
Spinning no more
Constant color of blues
Ocean of life
Fire in the skies
Beings from another world,
And Then the Angel appeared...

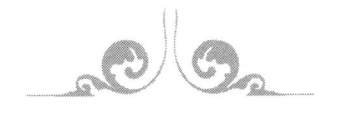

Sunshine of My Heart

Sing to me your loving song,
Wet my lips with yours,
Walk along the beach with me
Let us look up to the stars,
Light in your eyes more blue then
The skies showing me the way to
Your heart,
Dance with me in the clouds
Write me a poem,
Share your vows until Death do we part..
Through storms we will go knowing
Clear days are ahead having to struggle
With Cold dark moments wanting more
Than we have, Soon we will
Have instead of not we must trust
Ourselves and each other,
But mainly God...
For you my Queen is my life!
KIRA—The sunshine of my heart...

James R. Saner II

Sure of One Thing

And I am sure of one thing,
That a kiss is not just a kiss,
That the way you touch your spouse isn't
The way you touch a stranger
That beauty is in the soul not the body
And I am sure of one thing,
That when I forgive you it is worse
Than when I don't,
And I am sure of one thing,
You are the one who judges yourself,
Pain is feeling and feelings show caring
And if you are feeling then you are loved
Because sometimes the world is tough,
And I am sure of just one more thing,
I have yet to figure this life out.
Love is real Truth and that is Pain…

That's All

Little is said for growing older and
Having your money spent before you ever
Make it. Mouths to feed daily, dogs and
Cats, Little children sometimes little
Brats, Wife who's pregnant with your second
Child only working part time, doing her best
So she says don't have time to believe her.
Mortgage on a house, Car payments for both
Vehicles, Plus all the insurance Health,
Life, and Auto. Single Income Taxed by
The Government for their portion of what
I make, mistake speeding in a school zone
Officer just doing her job court costs and
Violation costs, Double it. All this
We pay Before we ever earn it, Little is
said for growing old, I'm only 21.
Word to the wise from the wise—— That's all.

James R. Saner II

The Altar

I walked into a dark and quiet church,
Seeking the sanctuary of faith, hope, love
Walking my way down the isle in search of
the altar, Going to kneel before the throne
Ask for guidance Direction,
When I came to the place where the altar
used to be, I found it empty
Just a set of steps going up to the stage
Where the Pastor speaks and the chorus sings
No lights just the gentle amber from glass
in the doors going outside, just enough
vision to see my way to the piano
Sit for a spell praying this way with the
white and black notes
Praise and Worship to the Creator of all this,
Playing to an empty audience
Nobody home. I'll come back later...
I left just as lost as when I had entered
the house. God help us all...

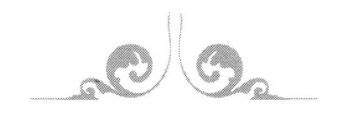

The Dark Temple

In the cracks you can feel the light
going out,
The dark temple with whispers heard
after hours
Laughs and shouts of pain
emptiness, Long and forever
The light just escapes the cold shadows
The dark temple with endless chills
Separation from all that is and was holy
not even the color black dwells there
The abyss with no light of fire
or warmth of body
The dark temple deserted
for worthless dreams and ambitious lust
Circle upon circle of a dizzying maze
Going on forever with no rest
or sense of peace
Just eluding the soul for eternity,
The dark temple never sees morning
or grace...

James R. Saner II

The Days Divide

Faith
Brought the day sun out to shine
She danced the sweet divine,
Rivers of madness
Sadness flowed
It can't be
Tormented again if it won't
Hope
Cast the moon into cycles
not letting it be full
For more than awhile
Breath easy the bird flies
High through the skies
Preying on another's soul
But look there
Do you see
The days divide???

Road to Reflection

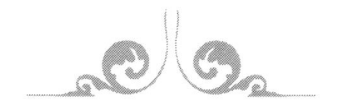

The Eve of New Beginnings

Wishing beyond fate to go back and try
Again to correct the unforeseen mistakes,
Life has few knowings, but many out comes,
Perfect in imperfection, Heart only beats
So fast, So many times, then one day it stops
So we can only promise to do our best and try
To maintain a true course,
Let us learn from
The lessons experienced, Bloody mess,
Standard is limitless, things must end
Hopefully not always bad,
We will carry on whether we like to or not
Such is living,
To begin again is Death...

James R. Saner II

The Foundation of God's House

The foundation of God's house
The like minded
The poor and rich both coming together
Black and white communion
The vision of hope
The simple answer to so much hurt,
So simple in fact
It just might work,
By faith I have seen it,
By will, I will share it
Choice there isn't one.
I am speaking of the youth and the aged both
To all really
A message of Trust
A tool for fellowship
out reach to the ones we know or think need such,
One house at a time in the ghetto minds the Projects
Need a leader...

Road to Reflection

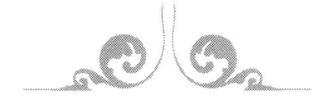

The Foundation of God's House continued...

Communities taking one family.
Going into that home and fixing what needs fixing.
One house at a time,
You will be surprised by the neighbors who come by asking and wondering what it is about.
A waking connection
A dream given a birth and life to grow
Becoming
deserving the right to feel good about themselves.
One house at a time
One heart becomes many,
The Projects need resurrection and love
The color blind dream is spoken.
It is not about one house over another house,
But the foundation of God's house
Which is the Human Heart.

James R. Saner II

The Free Mind

When I am born
I will share a tale with you,
I will speak to the Hearts of man
And connect with his spirit
Hers is not so far from home,
A timed death
She is killing herself
To bring me into this world
Refresh for me the things I believe
And the things I wish to
Confess
This life
Known as my Death is growing to a conclusion
Places everyone
For the show is formed
Way down deep inside the soul
There is light
Life of a new Kingdom

Road to Reflection

The Good News

The Dawn of a new year
Morning glory,
Sun rising Hot in its dance of wake
Sing the songs of the ancient ones
Birds fly high to the West,
Dance the deviled dance of Freedom
Cummed in my pants again,
Did you really get me off,
You wicked Demon, Legion of doom
Rebel of the forbidden moon
The crow speaking in volumes to come again,
I must approach this Great troubled time
With the hope that Tomorrow will be better.
This year of passion birthed into this world
From time or the spaces that it fills
To bring cleansing and refresh us
Washed in the river
Baptismal,

James R. Saner II

The Vision of Faith

Blast through the past to get
Here where we are,
Touched by the love of all
The vision of faith takes me
home.
Will we live to see forever?
Will we have the things we think we
Own?
Death like a shadow whispers
in the ears of all— sharing the fate
Sure to come,
One nation under God
and One nation that doesn't stop!
We will not rest until the job is done,
You can take that to your grave-

Road to Reflection

This Day

In this time of the Lord
Breath his spirit into my heart,
God,
Yes son, I love you...
Father I proclaim this day to you
I honor you this day,
I praise you this day,
I thank you this day,
And I do
I worship you this day.
Drink of the Lamb for
He is holy...

James R. Saner II

Those Who Dare Trespass

Shattered doors of time, Rhyme a new story
Cities being built Circled dwellings
Shape shift visions, Future does happen
The dream breathing life into old bones
Light happening, Over there
Dawns Horizon, Scattered highways
Walking barefooted
Night cap eagle dancing among the clouds
A top the totem
Resting with the wolf's pack
Howling to the moon
Bear stands two legged
Marking the trees
Giving warning to
those who dare trespass
I AM Going
The sin as it happens intrusion of private
Space
Fences marking grounds
NO body owns....

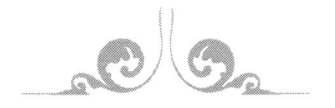

Till Your Fingers Hurt

A place I go inside myself
Music like a mountain spring going straight
toward the Delta Coast on through the muse
Continues to mock shock entice me
Play on journey of madness never ending
Sadness, Listen to the music of my soul
Blues, To nice a color Brother I have none
Band keeps playing on Just a little tune
Never able to play it again
Sick of these boots,
A waste of talent on this fool
Why God Why Me, Boo who boy
Take your toy, Your instrument and play Man play
Till your fingers hurt and Your thing goes soft
Lose it and Find what you lost awhile ago
Soul comes a knocking at my door
Voices soft and silent
The applause was short lived
Only one Fan...
A single shout "I WANT TO HEAR MORE"

James R. Saner II

To Be Healed

Ghost dancing alone
In circles, Power enhanced vision
The life after death Angels bring comfort,
Peaceful hands placed on shoulders
Whispers from a voice so quiet
Be blessed. Teachings of ancient healings
And Travel, Mind picks up the signal.
The body takes shape, Spirit
Holy Ghost awakens
Cries of the oooooommmmmm
Universal glue, Universal breath
Calling on the Gods of makeshift
Rise inside the temple…
Be reborn in this place
Take life a new in this vessel
I understand Now the things I have seen
I understand the message
To be healed you must accept…
There is Truth greater than we know
Who am I? I AM…

To Be Your Dad is Special

Your smile
Your kiss
Your sweetness
Tells me I am loved,
Your smile
Your kiss
Your sweetness
Tells me I am loved,
To be your Dad is special
To watch you grow and play,
There is nothing better in this
World than to be your Dad this day,
Your smile
Your kiss
Your sweetness
Tells me I am loved.

James R. Saner II

Too Long in The Low Hills

Dwelt to long in the low hills between the worlds,
I walk beyond them now into the future's past
To catch a glimpse of something to remember,
I faced her then in a time forgotten
She danced the better dance and sang
The song of the ages
Cast me away in a wind current to travel now
And then
I am again in the right kind of mind
Can feel the walls of my brain growing tighter
The pressure is building
I think it might blow
Yet then I become normal
I gain a new kind of Freedom
I then dance again with the maiden

Wake Up

If I wake from this dream
To find that all was for nothing
A second
a brief glimpse of a world I thought of
To have grown up
Had children
worked hard for (day in and day out)
married and had a wife
passion and true love
sacrifice blood, sweat, tears
gained a fortune
Played on the piano (gift from above)
So real and yet it's not... (wake up)

James R. Saner II

War Cry

Calling out to the warriors of
This tribe bring forth the whiteness
Gather the soul wisdom of the wakeful
Sleep no more for the passage has been
Opened, the anti-Christ is alive,
The lives of the children are at stake
Pray for the ancient God of ours to
Realize his is made and come forth
To reign.
All names be praised,
Sing from the heart the temple of
The most high God.

Washed

Expected, Accepted, Arms of love,
To hold the whole world at peace
Love come with us into the dreams we have
seen, The never ending sleep
To awake again refreshed & reborn
Nights cycle of Holy movement to interrupt
the day Bringing rest and relief
Our battles fought in season
Reclaim the night in our perfect legend
Depth of soul Never ending
The waters run off in rotation
Transforming in light and meditation
Revisited the same Mountain's top
Melting away into the lakes,
The arms reach out through the rivers,
Streamed back into ourselves,
Quenching thirst and constantly bathing (US)
I am cleansed by the water in my blood,
I have been to the other-side
And Back again

James R. Saner II

Ways of Power

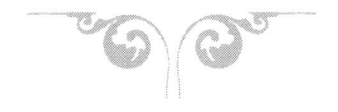

What of feeling and trust
What of the Host who
Is and Is not
Power of the Dream
Becoming a great Dreamer
To find the path of the One,
Be eaten by the Eagle
Everything and nothing
Death and life
Choice
Chosen,
Ways of Power
Beyond right here
Spirit does strange things to the chosen
One of its lineage
Give and Receive...

Road to Reflection

We Forgot

Let's see the full moon rise
watch as the waters change their motion
catch a glimpse of the universe and its
movement
stand still just long enough to be
filled with the quite noise and feel
the earth move and you with it constant
tides just along for the ride
spinning and spinning round & round
we have come and gone before but now
look see the door, locked
just for a moment
a single thought
we might have had the answers
we forgot...

James R. Saner II

Welcome the Damned

Moved with force of aging,
The plates shift opening spaces
To be filled with life source liquid
Massive change to the environment
Clouds of ash and gas to kill the
Breath seekers haunted with a gasp
For something of fresh air to inhale
The kingdom crashing before you
With wisdom and torture the ringing of the
Ears to be the end of us
To be sure enough it has only begun
We run into the night with screams of a
Child calling for its loved ones
Gentile I say Gentile do you really think
Your are chosen?
In this Eternal Nation
Welcome the Damned,
To be cleansed by the blood-
Live well then face the one
You proclaimed to be.

Road to Reflection

Well Paved & Open

To forget the program the work it takes,
to change, to accept something new and maybe
A little different. From Frost we see the
world and its characters as eternal written
in some bodies notebook, scrolls of the Holy
Ones who we reflect in memories of a dyeing
world, That one man can't leave a path for
Going on three millennium, saying that he will
return, somehow some way and that we would
know of his arrival, the King of the Jews
The Son of God, God himself in his creations
form, His image burns on the cross—
The Road to Heaven you must understand
is well paved and open to all who chose to
partake in its travel.

James R. Saner II

What I Think It Is...

In the light I have found darkness
And in the darkness I have found light
In motion I am and am not,
Creation of a time, place, faceless person.
lonely but not alone, company
I have enjoyed yours, Temple
The only one walks with you
Death brings life and life brings Death
confess and be forgiven,
take shape my house and my vessel
Ready for the wars to be over
Ready for the creation to continue
To imagine beyond this and know the journey
Is not yet at its end
I have found heaven or what I think it is...

World Order

Great is the maker creator of all this!
Pray on the world order and maybe
Please may I have a cheeseburger
Deadly enemy to our great country we
See them trying to sneak in and take over,
Trust us they say. Let us spend instead
Of save can we say slaves.
Who do you think created governments?
The Order is on our money and in our
Treasurer's top left hand drawer.
O you sneaky Devils
Legion is making its way into power.
Let us not talk of World Wars any more
But let us take a look at
Universal activity
and see the rise in the Heavens then the
Fall of theirs... Their going too, because
there is only One God.. Be with you!

James R. Saner II